Key Stage 3 RE
Morality

Christianity in Close-up

BOOK 3

Juliana Gilbride
Heather Hamilton

Colourpoint
Educational

© Juliana Gilbride, Heather Hamilton
and Colourpoint Books 2009

ISBN: 978 1 904242 98 7

First Edition
First Impression

Layout and design: Colourpoint Books
Printed by: GPS Colour Graphics Ltd

The acknowledgements on page 126 constitute an
extension of this copyright page.

The New International Version of the Bible has been used
throughout, unless otherwise stated.

Colourpoint Books
Colourpoint House
Jubilee Business Park
21 Jubilee Road
Newtownards
Co Down
BT23 4YH

Tel: 028 9182 6339
Fax: 028 9182 1900
E-mail: info@colourpoint.co.uk
Web site: www.colourpoint.co.uk

Juliana Gilbride BEd (Hons), MEd has fifteen years
experience of teaching Religious Studies to 'A' level
in Northern Ireland. She has also worked for Queen's
University, Belfast as a tutor on the PGCE course for
Religious Studies. She is a Principal Examiner for CCEA's AS
Religious Studies and a Reviser for CCEA's GCSE Religious
Studies.

Heather Hamilton BEd teaches Religious Education to
A2 level. She is Head of Religious Education in Omagh
Academy, County Tyrone, and has been teaching for
13 years. She is has worked as an Examiner for CCEA at
GCSE and 'A' level and is a Reviser for CCEA's GCSE Religious
Studies.

Contents

GUIDE TO ICONS

Activity

Discuss

Questions

Think

SKILLS AND CAPABILITIES KEY

Thinking Skills and Personal Capabilities*

Com Communication

ICT Using ICT

Ma Using Maths

MI Managing Information

BC Being Creative

TPD Thinking, Problem-solving, Decision-making

SM Self-management

WO Working with Others

Learning for Life and Work*

EfE Education for Employability

Cit Local and Global Citizenship

PD Personal Development

* These are suggestions only; you may be able to adapt activities further.

Self-Image

What does it mean to be unique?

Every day we are bombarded with pictures of famous people. We see them in magazines, on television, on the Internet and on billboard posters advertising perfume and clothes. The message is that we should try to be like them. If we want to 'fit in' and be popular then we need to look and act a certain way.

The Bible has a very different message. It teaches that each of us is unique. We are all different and can be proud of that fact. It states that God loves us no matter how we view ourselves.

The Bible also teaches that we should treat other people with respect and kindness, even though they might look very different to us. We need to accept people who don't wear the same clothes as us or listen to popular music, people from other countries and people with severe disabilities.

What is Self-Image?

An image can take a number of different forms. It might be a picture or drawing of an object or person; a reflection of a face in a mirror or a mental picture created by words. If you hear the word 'dog', an image will form in your mind of what that dog looks like. You might have in mind a small cute dog or perhaps a large ferocious one!

Self-image is the impression or picture that we have of ourselves. When we think about our appearance, what image forms in our mind? When we think about our talents and academic achievements, what words come to mind? Self image is our mental picture of who we are as complete individuals.

One of the most famous teachings of Jesus is to treat others as you would want to be treated. This can be a difficult lesson to learn. We might feel reluctant to accept certain members of society. We might disagree with their beliefs or feel threatened by their opinions.

TPD

In **Luke 10:27**, we are told to 'Love your neighbour as yourself'.

1 What do you think these words mean?

2 When Jesus uses the word 'neighbour', does he just mean the people who live next door to your house?

3 Can you think of any reasons why it would be difficult to love your 'neighbour'?

4 If everyone lived according to this saying, would the world be a better place, or a worse one?

The dictionary defines **unique** as:

Being the only one of a particular type.

In this crowded street, every individual is different and unique, but they are each still part of the human race.

BC
SM

Making A Snowflake

You might have heard in science class that no two snowflakes look the same. Scientists have spent years performing experiments to prove this theory, but we can find out the answer much more quickly.

Instructions for making a snowflake:

- Collect a sheet of blank A4 paper and a pair of scissors from your teacher.
- Using a pencil, lightly draw a circle on the page.
- Carefully cut out the circle using a pair of scissors.
- Fold the circle in half three times until it looks like a wedge of cheese.
- Around all three edges, carefully cut out simple shapes.

- When you are done, unfold the paper to reveal your snowflake!

When you have finished, compare your snowflake with those made by your classmates. Can you find one which is identical to your own?

The answer is likely to be **no**. Although there will be some similarities, no snowflake will be exactly alike.

The same could be said for each of the people in your class. Although you and your friends might all have the same colour of hair or like the same music, you are not identical. **Each of you is special in your own way**.

Com
WO

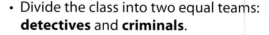

In pairs, discuss any similarities that you notice between the towers.

When you have finished, discuss what is different about them.

These towers have several things in common. For instance, they are all found in Europe and are important historical landmarks in their respective countries. However, they are all entirely unique.

What similarities and differences are there between people in your class?

MI
SM

Thumbprints

If you want proof that you are unique, you only need to look at your fingerprints. They will definitely be different from the fingerprints of everyone else in your class.

Each of us has a unique fingerprint. In fact, not even identical twins have the same fingerprints!

For this reason the police use fingerprints as a way of identifying criminals. You might have seen in a television show how detectives put a thief's fingers into ink and then press them onto paper. They compare these prints with those left behind at a crime scene. These prints are later used as evidence

in a court, and in many cases are enough to make a conviction.

- Divide the class into two equal teams: **detectives** and **criminals**.
- Using paint or an ink pad, each criminal makes a thumbprint on individual sheets of paper.
- The prints should be shuffled and given out to the detectives.
- It is the detectives' job to match the thumbprint to the criminal.

Thumbprint

In the heel of my thumb
are whorls, whirls, wheels
in a unique design:
mine alone.
What a treasure to own!
My own flesh, my own feelings.
No other, however grand or base,
can ever contain the same.
My signature,
thumbing the pages of my time.
My universe key,
my singularity.
Impress, implant,
I am myself,
Of all my atom part I am the sum.
And out of my blood and my brain
I make my own interior weather,
my own sun and rain.
Imprint my mark upon the world,
Whatever I shall become.

by Eve Merriam

From 'A Sky Full of Poems' by Eve Merriam. Copyright 1964, 1970, 1973, 1986 by Eve Merriam. Used by permission of Marian Reiner.

Read the following verses and think about what they suggest about your unique human identity:

'For you created my inmost being;
you knit me together in my mother's womb.
I praise you because I am fearfully and
wonderfully made;
your works are wonderful,
I know that full well.'

(Psalm 139:13-14)

Com
MI
WO

In pairs, discuss the following questions:

1 What do you think the poet means by the words, 'My universe key, my singularity'?

2 What does this poem teach us about our identity?

3 What is the author saying through this poem? Do you agree?

4 What would life be like if we were all exactly the same?

Christians believe that each individual person is a 'one off' model, a 'special edition' limited to one. We all have different personalities and identities, and we are all designed by God with a specific purpose.

MI
SM
PD

To show that you are unique, try comparing yourself with one of your brothers or sisters. If you are an only child (you really are unique!), compare yourself with a friend.

	Me	My brother / sister / friend
Name		
Height		
Birthday		
Eye colour		
Hair colour		
Hobbies		
Likes to eat		
Favourite music		
Likes to watch		

Though there will be some crossover between you and your sibling or friend, it is highly unlikely that you will get the exact same answers for both columns.

Body, Mind and Spirit

A chemist once analysed the human body and found that it is made from the most surprising stuff. The list reads more like a recipe than a biology report. Every living person contains:

- Enough fat for seven bars of soap.
- Enough iron for a medium-sized nail.
- Enough water to fill five buckets.
- Enough phosphorus to make the tips for 2000 matches.
- Enough lime to whitewash a hen house.
- Enough carbon for 9000 pencils.

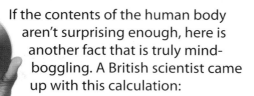

If the contents of the human body aren't surprising enough, here is another fact that is truly mind-boggling. A British scientist came up with this calculation:

During **80 years** the human brain processes **10 terabytes** of information. That is the equivalent of the storage capacity of **20,000 compact discs**!

Are human beings more than the chemicals we are made up of? Are we more than the information our brains hold?

There are some who argue that we are nothing more than physical beings, that there is no such thing as a **soul**, and that there is no **afterlife** to go to when we die.

Many people are not content with this view. They argue that there is a **spiritual** side to existence and that we must look for meaning in this life and beyond it. They believe that, as amazing as our brains are, there is more to being human than simply processing information. We are not computers performing the same tasks day in, day out. The Bible teaches that we have the capacity to think for ourselves, make choices that are good or bad, and control our lives as we see fit.

MI / SM / PD

What is Spiritual?

On a sheet of paper draw a large copy of this diagram.

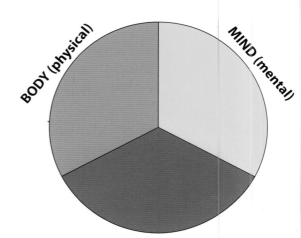

BODY (physical)

MIND (mental)

SPIRIT (spiritual)

Read each of the statements below, then write them into the appropriate section.

For example, "I believe in God" would go in the section marked "Spirit".

I believe in God.	**I think about a lot of things.**
I have dark hair.	**I worry about schoolwork.**
I am tall.	**I am good at Maths.**
I go to church.	**I love my friends.**
I have blue eyes.	**I wonder how the world began.**
I am a fast runner.	**I don't believe in God.**

Draw another copy of the diagram and complete it to describe yourself.

TPD / SM / Cit / PD

What are you worth?

The chemicals that make up a human body could be bought for around £3.00.

Is a human being worth more than that?

What is it that gives human beings value?

Who am I?

I'm boy and child and brother and son
Him over there, the poetry one
Passport holder 41604
I'm all of these things, and much much more.

I'm legs and arms and body and head
A weight that makes a dip in the bed
A size that stands in front of your door
I'm all of these things, and much much more.

I'm skin and bone and muscle and brain
A pumping heart, a feeler of pain
A bundle of cells with ME at the core
I'm all of these things, and much much more.

I'm every thought that rises and falls
The face that stares from mirrors on walls
A secret code passed down from before
I'm all of these things, and much much more.

by Steve Turner

Taken from 'Dad You're not Funny' by Steve Turner
(Lion Publishing plc, 1999. Copyright 1999 Steve Turner).

MI
TPD
SM

Re-read the poem carefully and answer the following questions:

1 Do you think that 'Who am I?' is a good title for the poem?

2 Can you think of another title for it?

3 What does the poet mean when he refers to himself as a 'bundle of cells' and a 'secret code'?

4 Which phrase is repeated throughout the poem. Why do you think it is repeated?

5 Why is ME written in capital letters?

6 Do you think that this poem has an important message? If so, what is it?

Com
SM
WO
PD

Get into **pairs**. Each of you should write a few paragraphs describing yourself in detail. You might want to think about:

- Your physical appearance
- Personality
- Hobbies and interests
- Likes and dislikes

When you are finished, read your description aloud to your partner. Take a few minutes to ask your partner what they thought of it. Was your description accurate?

In particular, try to think about which aspects you focused on most:

- Your physical appearance or your personality?
- Your negative or your positive qualities?

When you have finished, try writing a few paragraphs in which you describe your partner. Read it aloud to them when you have finished.

How does the description written by your partner compare with the one you wrote about yourself?

Self-Esteem

The French author Honoré de Balzac wrote:

'Nothing is a greater impediment to being in good terms with others than being ill at ease with yourself.'

Com
WO
PD

In pairs, take a few moments to consider the following questions:

1 What do you think Honoré de Balzac's words mean?

2 Do you agree with them? Why would our feelings about ourselves affect how we deal with others?

Some people find it difficult to respect others because they do not respect themselves. This is called **low self-esteem** - having a low opinion of yourself or feeling that you are worthless.

Everyone can struggle with feelings of low self-esteem at times. It is important that we deal with them properly or they can bother us all our lives. It also helps us to accept and get on well with others if we can accept who we are.

Talk to someone

The best thing you can do if you are struggling with low-self esteem is to talk to a trusted adult. Some people may find it too hard to talk to someone they know but there are lots of organisations which exist to help teenagers deal with their feelings.

One example is ChildLine, a free counselling service for children and teenagers.

You can call You can call ChildLine, the UK's free, confidential 24-hour helpline for children and young people on **0800 1111**.

ICT
SM
Other than ChildLine, what other organisations exist to help teenagers struggling with issues including low self-esteem?

People with low self-esteem struggle to believe that anybody would love them for who they are, even God. Yet, Christians believe that God does indeed love everybody. God sees each of us as uniquely made and we are incredibly important to God.

Com
BC
SM
WO
PD

Positives and Negatives

Get into groups of **six**.

Part A

- Place your hand on a blank piece of paper.
- Draw around your hand using a felt tip pen.
- Write your name beside the outline of your hand.
- On the fingers and thumb, write down **five** positive things about yourself.

Part B

- Take a new blank piece of paper.
- Place your hand on the page and draw around it.
- This time the paper will be passed around your group.
- Each person in your group should write down **one** positive thing about you in your fingers and thumb.

As a class, discuss which task you found more difficult: **Part A** or **Part B**. Explain why.

Perhaps negative self-image made part A difficult. Similarly with part B, we can find it embarrassing when other people focus on us.

The Dalai Lama, a Buddhist teacher, once said, 'If you don't love yourself, you cannot love others', but what does 'loving yourself' mean? Here are some options:

- A **narcissistic** person loves and admires their appearance so much that they become completely self-absorbed. The word 'narcissistic' comes from the name Narcissus, a character in Greek mythology who fell in love with his own reflection in a pool of water. Narcissus was preoccupied with himself and neglected everyone else in his life.

- An **egoistic** person is selfish and always puts his or her needs before those of others. Such a person believes that their personal happiness is all that matters.

- The ideal is to have **healthy and realistic self-esteem**. You should be able to recognise your strengths and weaknesses, and accept your positive and negative qualities.

TPD
PD

From the following list choose **five** words that you feel best sum up how young people feel about the changes that adolescence brings. Give reasons for your choices.

Awkward	**Frightened**
Happy	**Shy**
Confused	**Self-conscious**
Emotional	**Excited**
Confident	**Nervous**
Angry	**Sad**

Com
WO

As a class, discuss if there is a difference between loving yourself and being self-centred.

A group of young people were asked how it feels to be teenagers rather than children. Here is a selection of their replies:

'It's difficult as people expect more from you.'

Adolescence and being yourself

Sometimes it is difficult to be content with who you are. Teenage years can be a time of great insecurity and anxiety. As you grow from a child into an adult, you change both physically and emotionally. Loneliness, fear and uncertainty are feelings common to most teenagers, even those who appear confident on the surface. You might feel self-conscious but not be entirely sure why. Surges of hormones can cause mood swings that are confusing and difficult to cope with.

'I have more rows with my mum and dad.'

'I have so many questions. It's confusing.'

'It's great. I have so much more independence and confidence.'

Some teenagers find it hard to know who they really are. Instead they try to become what they think others expect them to be. They feel that to be accepted and loved they must wear certain clothes or trainers, go to particular places or socialise with the popular people from their school. Sometimes this leads them into doing things they should not be doing.

This is often the result of **insecurity**. It's said that people change their outside when they are not happy with the way they feel on the inside.

Unreality

In this mechanical world of
false eyelashes,
false teeth,
contact lenses,
fantastic face lifts,
eye-deceiving hair pieces and surgically removed bulges –
please help me to become
what eternity planned me to be.
For I suspect that striving to be
what I am not
is little more than symptoms
of insecurity with what I am.

by Phil Streeter

Taken from *The Divinity of Daydreams* (1986)

Com **MI** **WO**

In pairs, discuss the following questions. When you are finished, share your ideas with the rest of the class.

1 What do you think the poet is trying to say in 'Unreality'? Why do you think he wrote this poem?

2 Many people feel under pressure to conform to the crowd and loose their uniqueness. Where do you think this pressure comes from? Make a list of your ideas.

The Book of Proverbs is a collection of wise sayings in the Bible.

In **Proverbs 22:6** we read:

'Train a child in the way he should go and when he is old he will not turn from it.'

Here, the writer says that a child raised with good morals is more likely to hold onto those standards in later life.

Anne Frank writes in her famous diary:

'All children must look after their own upbringing. Parents can only give good advice or put them on the right paths, but the final forming of a person's character lies in their own hands.'

Parents, teachers and other authority figures can support teenagers to guide them along the right path, but in the end each individual is responsible for their own behaviour.

Com **TPD**

Discuss as a class:

Look again at the two quotations above. Which statement do you agree with more? Proverbs or Anne Frank?

TPD **PD**

Look at the three pictures below.

1 Is the glass half full or half empty?

2 Is the burger half eaten or is half of it still left?

3 Is the homework good because it is an improvement or is it poor because it could be better?

Think carefully about your responses to these questions.

• Were your answers positive or negative?

• What do your responses tell you about how you think about things?

Com
WO

In pairs, read the poem below and discuss how it makes you feel.

Today upon a bus, I saw a lovely girl
with golden hair;
I envied her – she seemed so happy – and
wished I were as fair.
When suddenly she rose to leave, I saw
her hobble down the aisle;
She had one foot and wore a crutch, but
as she passed, a smile.
Oh, God, forgive me when I whine;
I have two feet – the world is mine!

And then I stopped to buy some sweets.
The lad who sold them had
such charm, I talked with him – he said to me:
'It's nice to talk with folks like you.
You see,' he said, 'I'm blind.'
Oh, God, forgive me when I whine;
I have two eyes – the world is mine!

Then, walking down the street, I saw
a child with eyes of blue.
He stood and watched the others play;
it seemed he knew not what to do.
I stopped for a moment, then I said:
'Why don't you join the others, dear?'
He looked ahead without a word, and then
I knew he could not hear.
Oh, God, forgive me when I whine;
I have two ears – the world is mine!

With feet to take me where I'd go,
with eyes to see the sunset's glow,
with ears to hear what I would know,
oh, God, forgive me when I whine;
I'm blessed, indeed! The world is mine.

Anonymous

Taken from *Assemble Together 2* by Tony Castle
(Kevin Mayhew Ltd, 2001).

Letter To Your Future Self

Com
BC
SM

If you could write a letter to yourself in the future, what would you say?

Collect a sheet of writing paper and an envelope from your teacher. You are going to write a letter that is only to be read when you are **21**.

Your letter should describe what you think of your life now and what you hope your will be like in the future.

Think about what you would like to achieve by that age. It may help you to make a list. Here are some things you might want to think about:

• Will you be married?

• Will you be at university or working?

• Will you be rich?

• Will you still be at home or travelling the world?

Seal the letter in the envelope and write ' To be opened on my 21st Birthday' on the front. No peeking!

Definitions

MI
SM

Look back through this chapter and give definitions of the following words and phrases:

• Unique

• Self-image

• Spiritual

• Low self-esteem

Created in the Image of God

Christians believe that the universe and everything in it was designed and created by God. This includes our planet and all the animals and human beings who live here.

James Weldon Johnson writes about this in his poem 'The Creation'.

The Creation

Then God sat down
On the side of a hill where he could think;
By a deep, wide river he sat down;
With his head in his hands,
God thought and thought,
Till he thought, I'll make me a man!
Up from the bed of the river
God scooped the clay;
And by the bank of the river
He kneeled him down;
And there the great God Almighty
Who lit the sun and fixed it in the sky,
Who flung the stars to the most far corner of the night,
Who rounded the earth in the middle of his hand;
This great God,
Like a mammy bending over her baby,
Kneeled down in the dust
Toiling over a lump of clay
Till he shaped it in his own image;
Then into it he blew the breath of life,
The man became a living soul.
Amen. Amen.

by James Weldon Johnson

In **Genesis 1:27** we read:

> 'So God created man in his own image, in the image of God he created him; male and female he created them.'

Com
MI
TPD

Christians believe that each individual is made in the image of God, but what does this mean?

Choose **four** statements that you think explain the idea of the image of God and write them down in your classwork book.

1 God is a giant who sits around up in the clouds all day long.

2 Human beings look like God.

3 Humans have the potential to be as powerful as God.

4 Everyone has a spiritual part of their personality and can form a close relationship with God.

5 Humans can live forever with God.

6 If humans want to find God they should look within themselves.

7 Humans have the potential to be creative.

8 Humans share some of God's characteristics such as the ability to love, forgive and express anger.

Now, discuss your ideas with a partner.

TPD

Look at this picture by the famous artist Michelangelo. What do you think he is trying to show in this picture?

The Value of Human Life

Christians believe that God loves everybody equally and that God's love doesn't depend on abilities, birthplace, intelligence, skin colour, health or age. They argue that God designed and created each of us for a particular purpose.

MI
SM
Cit

Read these passages and answer the following questions:

'Your hands made me and formed me; give me understanding to learn your commands. May those who fear you rejoice when they see me, for I have put my hope in your word.'

(Psalm 119:73-74)

'Are not five sparrows sold for two pennies? Yet not one of them is forgotten by God. Indeed, the very hairs of your head are all numbered. Don't be afraid; you are worth more than any sparrows.'

(Luke 12:6-7)

1 What does the Bible say about the value of human life?

2 Christians believe that life is **sacred**. What does this mean? Look the word up in a dictionary if you are stuck.

3 How do you think this belief affects how Christians think about such issues as abortion, suicide and euthanasia?

Not everyone agrees about the value of human life. Some people judge certain groups, such as the disabled, the old, or the ill as less able and therefore of less value. These groups are often **marginalised** in our society – they are not treated with the same respect as those who are considered to be 'normal'.

One person who came to realise the true value of human life was **Hilary J Pole**. She had grown up just like any other child. When she was young she loved games and dancing. Later, she became a PE and dance teacher, where she was able to continue to follow her passion for physical activity.

Sadly, Hilary fell ill with a terrible disease. At first, it affected her hands, feet, arms and legs. She could feel, hear and speak, but she couldn't move these parts of her body. As time went on she was slowly paralysed to the point that she could not move her mouth or her eyelids.

Hilary could hear but she could not make any sound. She could not sing, dance or do any of the things that she loved. As she was unable to chew or eat, she was fed through tubes and kept alive with a breathing machine.

TPD
PD
How do you think you would feel if you were Hilary? What words would best sum up how she felt at this time in her life?

Hilary could only move a tiny part of her body: the big toe on her right foot. She slowly discovered that she could communicate by giving it a little flicker when she wanted to 'speak'.

At first, Hilary had to spell out words letter by letter. Three years later, she was helped enormously when she received a device called a Possum machine. This helped her to control switches, turn on the radio and, best of all, use a typewriter.

After several years of frustration, Hilary finally had a way to let out all of her emotions. In fact, once she started writing she found it difficult to stop. She wrote, amongst other things, poems and articles for magazines.

Hilary Pole died two years later during an operation, but her life story continues to inspire anybody who hears it. She was a courageous person who always had a positive attitude even during the toughest times.

The following poem is just one of many that Hilary J Pole wrote about her disability. Note how brave and content she sounds, in spite of her circumstances.

My Answer

I'm often asked if I am bored,
frustrated, lonely,
my life abhorred.
And so I answer,
'I am not'.
that now I can accept my lot,
remind the sadly shaking head,
'It is my body, not my mind, in bed'.

I'm rarely frightened or in pain,
for this
I thank my God again.
I have many loyal friends,
my joy in them despair transcends.
There's music, too,
books to read;
discontentment cannot breed.

Although I can no longer play,
I can listen
everyday
to football, rugby, tennis, cricket,
imagination has not limit.
Add to this
a sense of humour
killing that 'depression' rumour.

Now I have my Possum too,
a miracle
in all men's view.
No longer do I have to wait,
my poems and letters to dictate;
just flick my toe
and type myself –
I have no time to brood on 'health'!

by Hilary J Pole

Taken from Assemble Together by Tony Castle, 1999, (Kevin Mayhew Ltd., 1999)

Com
MI
WO
PD

Discuss the following questions in groups.

1 How did this poem make you feel?

2 Think of words which best describe what you think Hilary was like. You might think of words like **brave**, **afraid**, **happy**, **content** etc. Discuss each one and quote from her poem to show why your description is correct or incorrect.

3 Do you think that faith in God was important to Hilary?

4 Imagine that you are Hilary. You are asked whether or not you think that all human life is of equal value. How do you respond?

Com
BC

Write your own poem appreciating all the things that you can do: playing sport, going out with friends, going to school, taking your dog for a walk, swimming etc.

Respecting your body

The Bible contains many verses that encourage people to respect their bodies and look after them in a responsible way. **Genesis 1:31** states that when God created the world and human beings, he looked at his creation and was pleased with it.

Read the following passage, written by the Apostle Paul.

'Do you not know that your body is a temple of the Holy Spirit, who is in you, whom you have received from God? You are not your own; you were bought at a price. Therefore honour God with your body'

(**1 Corinthians 6:19-20**).

Verse 19 states that our bodies do not belong to us, but rather to God. Christians believe that their bodies are a gift from God; they are 'on loan', so they must be looked after and not abused.

TPD

What do you think Paul meant when he said that the human body is a like a temple?

Think about the purpose of a temple and how people might treat such a building.

Com
TPD
PD

Imagine that you have borrowed a DVD from a friend.

1 How do you treat it?

2 Do you take more or less care of than you do of your own DVDs?

3 How would you feel if you accidentally damaged it?

4 What would you do if this happened?

Share your answers with a partner and discuss:

If we treat our possessions carefully, then how much more carefully should you treat your own body?

Com
MI
TPD
SM
WO

Using and Abusing

A group of teenagers were asked to make a list of some of the ways people mistreat their bodies. Several suggested **smoking** and **taking drugs**, but there were various other replies.

1 What things would you add to the list? Take a few moments to write out some possible suggestions for the ways in which people mistreat their bodies.

2 Now rearrange the list by placing it in order, beginning with what you think is the worst abuse at the top, and the one that is least harmful at the bottom.

3 Compare your list with those written by your classmates. Discuss your choices.

• Did you all consider the same things to be the most harmful?
• What is it about these particular things that is so harmful?
• Did you all consider the same things to be the least harmful?
• Why are these things not considered to be as dangerous as other ones?

Com
TPD

Spectrum Debate

Create a line down the middle of your classroom. Mark one end 'strongly agree'. Mark the other end 'strongly disagree'. Mark the middle of the line 'not sure'.

Your teacher will read out the statements below.

Take a moment to think, then place yourself anywhere along the line according to how much you agree with the statement.

Be prepared to explain your position.

• People should treat their bodies with respect.
• Human beings are animals.
• Human beings have a spiritual side.
• The life of a dying criminal and the life of a new-born baby are of equal value.
• Human beings are made in the image of God.

Christians believe that God allows people to make their own choices in life. Some people choose to follow God and to seek God's guidance for how to live their lives. Others don't take God's word into account. This will effect how people treat their bodies: what they eat, what they drink, the amount of exercise they take etc.

Com
TPD
WO
PD

In groups, read the following passage and then discuss the questions at the end.

Kerry is thirty-five. She is married and has three young children, each of whom is under the age of eight. Kerry goes out every weekend with her friends for a meal, drinks and dancing, while her husband Alan stays at home and looks after the kids.

Kerry takes a taxi home alone because she lives in a different part of the city than her friends. She is quite frequently drunk when she arrives at the house.

Alan always waits up for Kerry. He tells her that he is worried about her safety and her health, but she tells him to stop nagging. 'I work hard to provide for this family,' she says. 'My job is very stressful so I deserve to let off steam every now and again. Besides, it's not doing anybody any harm.'

1 Do you agree with Kerry? Do you think she deserves to enjoy herself at the weekends?

2 Explain how other members of the family could be affected by her behaviour.

3 How might Kerry and her family be affected in the future?

Gender and Sexuality

Gender Roles

The book of Genesis tells us that God created both men and women in his image, but what does it mean to be male and female in our society? What sort of judgements and assumptions are made about men and women, or boys and girls?

Com
MI
SM

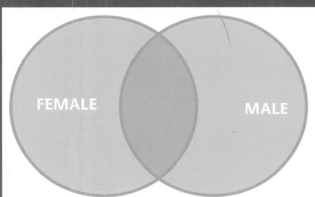

Copy out this diagram.

Look at the list of tasks carried out in a typical family home. Write the tasks usually performed by males into the right-hand circle and the tasks usually performed by females into the left-hand circle. Tasks that are shared should be written in the middle section.

- Ironing
- Sewing and mending
- Taking out the rubbish
- Changing a light bulb
- Making family appointments with the doctor or dentist

- Attending parent / teacher meetings
- Cooking
- Hoovering
- Helping with homework
- Cutting the grass
- Dusting

- Making beds
- Cleaning the windows
- Washing dishes / Loading dishwasher
- Changing a plug
- Decorating

Compare your sphere with two pupils near you. Do you notice any similarities or differences?

In recent years male and female roles, both inside and outside the home, have changed a great deal. Previously, certain jobs were done only by men and women were not allowed to do them. Likewise, other jobs were reserved for women only.

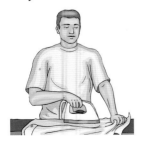

Com
TPD

Discuss the following questions as a class:

1 Would you buy a beautiful pink outfit for a newborn baby boy?

2 Should boys play a game of rugby with a girl?

3 Would you want to be treated by a male nurse in hospital?

4 Do you think that women should be able to join the army?

TPD / Cit / PD

1 Can you think of any jobs that **women** do today that they would not have done in the past?

2 Can you think of any jobs that **men** do today that they would not have done in the past?

MI / TPD / SM

Look closely at this photograph of a young woman and answer the following questions:

1 Describe her clothes. How are they different from modern clothes?

2 What do you think she is doing?

3 What do you think a typical day was like for her?

4 How does this woman compare to a young mother today?

5 What do you think life will be like in the future for the girls in your class?

A housewife in the 1930s

Gender Stereotyping

Even though things have changed a great deal, misconceptions still exist about what it means to be male or female. **Gender stereotyping** is when people assume certain things about an individual because of their gender, for example:

'He's a boy so he must like football.'

'She's a girl so she must like wearing pink dresses.'

The simple fact is that not all boys enjoy playing football and not all girls like wearing pink dresses. This is a basic example but it illustrates how we can make assumptions about someone's personality just because of their gender.

TPD / SM / WO / Cit / PD

Can you think of other stereotypes in our society?

List as many as you can, then compare your list with a partner.

Are any of your stereotypes similar? Do you disagree with any of the stereotypes on your partner's list?

There are some families who go against the stereotyped view of how a household should be run. In these houses, the women go out to work while the men stay at home as **house husbands**, looking after the family, cooking, cleaning, buying the groceries etc.

Jim is a **stay-at-home dad** whose wife Lisa works as a solicitor. They have three children together. When they had a family they decided that Jim would take care of the children while Lisa would remain working as she earns more money.

'It's not that we are being greedy. It's just that we have a big mortgage to pay so this seemed to be the best solution. Childcare is so expensive that it works out cheaper this way. I have to admit that there are times when I find it difficult, especially when the children are fighting. Lisa definitely seems to have more patience than me. I don't know if it's because she is a woman or because she gets away from them whenever she is at work!'

TPD

1 Do you think men should be prepared to stay at home to mind the children if their wife earns more money? Give reasons for your answer.

2 Why might some people disagree with what Jim and Lisa are doing?

3 What pressures will be on Jim and Lisa for making this choice?

4 Do you think that many men would be willing to give up their jobs to do this? If there are any boys in your class, take a vote to see how many of them would be happy to be a stay-at-home dad.

The Suffragettes

During the 1800s and 1900s many women in Great Britain and America campaigned for women's **suffrage** – the right to vote. Some were even sent to prison as a result.

In 1918, women in the UK were granted the right to vote. The USA followed in 1920.

Sexism

Sexism is when someone is treated unfairly because of their gender. For example, a man might be given less chance of getting a job normally given to women, or vice-versa.

In 1975, the **Sex Discrimination Act** was passed to protect people against discrimination on the basis of gender. This means that men and women can now work in the same jobs.

It was not always like this. You may have learnt in History that in previous centuries women were not viewed as equal to men, and they certainly did not have the same opportunities.

In the past, women were not allowed to vote or to work in the same jobs as men. In some cases women were not allowed to sit the same examinations as men. Since then, people have campaigned against these prejudices and women have gradually been given more respect and authority in society.

MI
TPD
SM

You have just become the principal of a school. You think that many of the school rules are old-fashioned and sexist. Here are a few examples: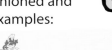

School Rules

1. Girls are not permitted to engage in physically demanding sports such as rugby, cricket and cross country running. These pursuits are unladylike, and are beyond the capabilities of female pupils.

2. During the summer term, female pupils may wear open-collared blouses with no tie. Male pupils must wear blazers when outdoors and be neatly presented at all times. The removal of ties is strictly prohibited.

3. Friday afternoon classes will be divided between Home Economics for girls and Technology for boys.

4. The weights in the gymnasium are only for use by boys fifth form and above.

5. Girls must wear skirts and boys must wear trousers.

- Are any of the rules acceptable?
- Rewrite the rules, making any changes you think will make the school more accepting and understanding.

ICT
MI
SM

Use the internet or a library to find out ways in which life has changed for women during the past 100 years. Make a list of them.

Com
TPD

Some people would argue, that while men and women should be treated fairly and equally, we also need to acknowledge that men and women are different. It could be said that more men tend to be natural leaders, and more women tend to be natural carers.

Therefore, it makes sense that men should go out to work while women stay at home to care for the house and the family.

Organise a class debate based on the following statement:

'Men are meant to be leaders and women are meant to be carers. That's the way we were designed.'

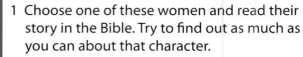

1 Choose one of these women and read their story in the Bible. Try to find out as much as you can about that character.

2 Put together a fact file on your chosen character. Tell a little of their story and include as much information about her as you can. Do you know:
  • What age they are?
  • If they are married?
  • If they have children?
  • What sort of relationship they have with God?
  • Why they are a famous character in the Bible?

3 Illustrate your fact file with a picture. You could draw your character, or you could make a collage out of magazine cuttings.

Women in the Bible

Some people argue that the Bible is sexist. God is referred to as 'he', stories sometimes show female characters to be cunning or cruel, and the main characters are usually men.

In the times and places that the Bible was written, men were usually in charge. A woman was viewed as the property of her father, and later her husband. This is still the case in some parts of the world.

Bearing that in mind, the Bible actually has a surprisingly large number of strong female characters.

ICT
MI
BC
SM

Here are just four examples of women in the Bible with extraordinary stories:

• Rahab (**Joshua 2**) stood up to the king of Jericho to protect two men.

• Deborah (**Judges 4-5**). A prophet and Judge of Israel, she led the people into battle.

• Ruth (**Ruth 1-4**) is so dedicated to her mother-in-law that she leaves her own country.

• Esther (**Esther 1-2**) influenced powerful leaders and saved her people from being wiped out.

At the time of Jesus it was considered shameful for a woman to talk to any man apart from her father, brothers or husband.

Jesus challenges the attitude of his society by talking to women in public, eating with them, and helping them with their problems. Many of Jesus' close friends were women. He was not afraid of being criticised for his actions.

TPD

Copy the table below and complete it, comparing how women were thought of in the time of Jesus with how they are thought of now.

In Jesus' time	Now
Women were seen as less important than men.	In most cases, women are seen as equal to men, but...
Women were not allowed to speak to men in public.	etc.
etc.	

When Jesus and his twelve disciples travelled around, a larger group travelled with them:

After this, Jesus travelled about from one town and village to another, proclaiming the good news of the kingdom of God. The Twelve were with him, and also some women who had been cured of evil spirits and diseases: Mary (called Magdalene) from whom seven demons had come out; Joanna the wife of Cuza, the manager of Herod's household; Susanna; and many others. These women were helping to support them out of their own means.

(Luke 8: 1-3)

Not only did Jesus have female followers, but it seems that they used their money to help Jesus. Later, when Jesus rose from the dead, the first people to see him were his female followers.

Hot Seat

Read **John 8:1-11**.

Here we read of a woman who was caught having an affair. This breaks the seventh of the Ten Commandments: 'You shall not commit adultery'. In the law of the time the penalty was stoning – people would throw rocks at her until she was dead.

The religious leaders bring her to Jesus and ask him what they should do. They wanted to trick Jesus. He would be forced to either condemn her to death, or go against the law.

Jesus' answer neither condemns the woman, nor goes against the law. In fact, the religious leaders all leave, and the woman is unharmed.

Place a seat at the front of the classroom.

Pick one person in the class to sit in the seat and play the role of the woman.

The rest of the class now think of questions to ask the character. For example;
- How are women treated, compared to men?
- How did you feel when the religious leaders started accusing you?
- Did you think you were going to die?
- What did you think when all the religious leaders walked away?
- What do you think of Jesus?

How would you have answered the questions differently?

Repeat the activity, this time with one of the religious leaders in the hot seat.

Com MI BC

Expressing our sexuality

Christians believe that sexuality is a gift from God and that it should be used wisely. Despite what you might have heard, the Bible is not against sex. In fact, it teaches that it is a natural part of being human. It also teaches that people should respect their sexuality and not misuse it.

Rules exist to keep people safe. For example, the Highway Code is there to help protect drivers and pedestrians. When people ignore it and follow their own rules on the road, this leads to accidents and injuries, some of which are fatal.

Similarly, the Bible gives advice for expressing human sexuality in the way that God intended. It offers a great deal of advice about how to behave in order to have successful relationships.

Christians normally take the view that sex is best when it takes place inside marriage. For this reason, most Christians choose to stay **celibate** – this means not engaging in sexual activity outside marriage. It is not only Christians who adopt this approach. Other people remain celibate for similar religious reasons, or simply because they agree with the principles.

Look up the verses below, and match them to the advice the Bible gives about developing a healthy attitude to sexuality.

1 Corinthians 6:13	Husbands and wives should be faithful to each other.
1 Corinthians 6:19	God's creation was perfect and living outside his rules leads to physical and emotional pain.
Proverbs 5:15	We should respect our bodies and use them to serve God.
Genesis 1:31	Humans are made in God's image and should respect themselves and others. They should never misuse another person.
Genesis 1:27	God created us, so our bodies are 'on loan' from him. People should not do anything to damage them.

The **Song of Songs** (or Song of Solomon) is a book of the Bible all about sexuality. It is a love poem between a young man and young woman. It begins:

> 'Kiss me again and again, for your love is sweeter than wine.'
>
> **(Song of Songs 1:2)**

The young woman realises how strong these feelings are, and warns her friends repeatedly:

> 'I want you to promise, O women of Jerusalem, not to awaken love until the time is right.'
>
> **(Song of Songs 8:4)**

At one time the Song of Songs was considered so unsuitable that young people were discouraged from reading it.

The Great Debate

Read the arguments for and against the Christian view of sexuality.

For

'Sex should definitely be kept for marriage. Having just one sexual partner is healthier, and it's romantic! It means that both partners are totally committed to each other. Also, marriage means the couple will be ready to have a baby.'

Against

'The Christian rules are outdated and irrelevant. People should be free to make up their own minds about whether they have sex or not. The idea of people waiting until they are married is old-fashioned. People need to know whether they are good together before they get married.'

- In pairs, pick one partner to argue 'for', and one to argue 'against'.
- Take a few minutes to write down some arguments that you are going to use. You can use the arguments above, and anything else you can think of.
- Take it in turns to argue as strongly as possible for your side.
- Now, switch places and repeat the process, this time arguing for the opposite view.
- Discuss what you personally think about each view. What were the strongest arguments?

Sexual Orientation

When someone speaks of their **sexual orientation** they mean the gender to which they are attracted. There are two different words for this:

Heterosexual means attraction to a member of the opposite sex.

Homosexual means attraction to a member of the same sex.

The majority of people are heterosexual. Like many **minority groups**, homosexual people occasionally experience hatred or abuse from others. This is called **homophobia**.

Did you know?

During the **Holocaust**, the Nazis tried to wipe out millions of people. As well as Jews, the Nazis also targeted Romani Gypsies, physically and mentally disabled people and homosexuals.

PD Sometimes phrases that could be very offensive to someone from a minority group can become accepted, particularly by young people.

Do you use any terms which could be hurtful to people from minority groups? Do you ever use any phrases which sound homophobic?

People often ask what the Church believes about homosexuality. It is difficult to answer this question satisfactorily as Christians disagree on this issue. Some are bitterly opposed to homosexuality, but others believe that homosexual people should be welcomed into the Church. Some argue that there should be nothing to stop homosexuals holding leadership roles in the Church and become priests or ministers.

MI
SM

You will hear many different views regarding homosexuality. Read the following statements and decide where you would place yourself on the scale for each one.

Strongly Disagree ← *Disagree* ← *Not Sure* → *Agree* → *Strongly Agree*

1 Homosexuality is completely wrong. It goes against God's will. God created man and woman to be together and homosexuality ignores this. It is unnatural and sinful.

2 If you have homosexual feelings it is not your fault. You do not choose to be that way. However, it is wrong to act upon these feelings by becoming involved in a homosexual relationship.

3 Homosexuality is simply a part of someone's identity. They are made that way. It is acceptable to have a homosexual relationship as long as it is with only one person and they are faithful to each other.

4 God loves and accepts us for who we are. This includes homosexuals. It is acceptable to be a practising homosexual and a Christian. Homosexual people should not be excluded from the Church.

What does the Bible say about homosexuality?

It teaches that God created men and women to be together and to become physically intimate within marriage. **Leviticus 18:22** warns male readers:

'Do not have sexual relations with a man as one does with a woman; that is detestable.'

In **1 Corinthians 6:9-10**, Paul states his opinion firmly:

'Do you not know that the wicked will not inherit the kingdom of God? Do not be deceived: Neither the sexually immoral nor idolaters nor male prostitutes nor homosexual offenders nor thieves nor the greedy nor drunkards nor slanderers nor swindlers will inherit the kingdom of God.'

These passages seem to state that homosexuality and Christianity are not compatible. However, some people disagree with this. They suggest that the Bible never talks about the kind of homosexual relationships that some people have today.

Others argue that it is more important to practise Jesus' command to love one's neighbour. They say that this instruction calls for the acceptance of all people, including homosexuals.

There is no doubt that Christians will continue to discuss the issue of how the Church should treat homosexuality.

What influences our sexual values?

Our **values** are our morals or beliefs, and we often feel uncomfortable when they are challenged. Many people have different values, which means that one person might find something perfectly acceptable whilst another will find it offensive and harmful.

For example, many people object to the way in which television, cinema and the media in general depict sex. Magazines frequently use photographs of a sexual nature to sell a particular product, and soap operas use controversial plots to increase ratings. Many parents worry how their children will be affected by the kind of images that are being thrown at them on a daily basis.

TPD	
WO	
Cit	
PD	

Work in pairs to make a list of the ways in which sexuality is presented in the media (television programmes, music, films, magazines, newspapers). Present this as a table.

In the left hand column list examples of:

• Storylines in soap operas and dramas involving sex and sexuality, particularly those involving young people.

• The lyrics to songs that are currently in the charts.

• News stories.

In the right hand column, explain what message each gives about sex, marriage and relationships.

How might these messages affect teenagers' attitudes towards sex?

Our values can be determined and affected by the world around us and that includes the magazines we read and television we watch. One of the problems with this is that sex is often treated lightly on television. The seriousness and specialness of sex is not clearly depicted and Christian values are rarely presented.

Have you ever heard the term '**casual sex**'? This is sometimes used to describe occasional sexual encounters purely for entertainment, with no basis in relationship.

Most people agree that sex is made for committed relationships. There is nothing casual about sex!

TPD
Cit
PD

What problems would be caused if someone's values towards sex were based entirely on soap operas?

Com
BC
WO
Cit
PD

In pairs, look through a range of magazines and newspapers, and think about the following questions:

1 How does the media use images of the human body to promote and sell products?

2 Are these images respectful or degrading?

3 Do you think that they have a positive or negative effect upon:
   a. The people who see them?
   b. The people in the pictures?

4 Do you think that these images create a careless attitude to sex?

Choose one advert and redesign it so it promotes the product without using sexual images.

How does it affect me?

Adolescence is a time during which many young people start to form close relationships with members of the opposite sex. It is important for teenagers to have clear sexual values so they will not make choices they may regret in the future.

During their teenage years young people can feel pressurised by their peers to become more experienced, but it is important to realise that sex is an issue that should be taken seriously.

Sexuality is an incredibly important part of being a human being. Sex shouldn't be treated lightly. Your sexual values are something that only you can decide.

BC
TPD
SM
PD

Points Of View

Craig and Stephanie are both fifteen years old. That have been boyfriend and girlfriend for two years and have known each other for much longer. Craig wants to take the physical side of the relationship further, but Stephanie isn't so sure.

List as many possible points of view for each of the following.

Craig
For example:
• 'We're old enough now.'
• 'There's no reason we shouldn't do it.'

Stephanie
For example:
• 'I'm not sure I want this.''
• I want Craig to be happy, but I'm not sure he's the right guy.

Stephanie's Dad:

The Law:

What do I look for?

There is more to every relationship than the physical side. Here is a list of some of the other qualities which someone might look for in a boyfriend or girlfriend:

fun to be with	**good looking**
honest	**makes me feel wanted**
intelligent	**phones me regularly**
easy to talk to	**has lots of money**
makes others jealous	**generous**
good at sport	**makes me laugh**
quiet and gentle	**similar interests to me**
never complains	**dresses well**

1 Make a personal list of the things that you would look for in a boyfriend or girlfriend. Use any of the points from the sample list and add others that are important to you.

2 Rank the points in order of importance, with 1 being the most important.

Right and Wrong and the Role of Conscience

Christians believe that God created human beings with **free will**. We are free to make our own decisions about what to believe and how to behave. What we decide about what is right and wrong will affect us individually, as well as our family and friends and our communities.

Decisions about what is right and what is wrong are not always simple. We all live in the same world but we do not all see it in the same way. One person might think that something is right but another person might think that the same thing is wrong.

TPD
SM

There are some issues where people disagree on whether it is right or wrong. For example, war or eating meat.

How many issues can you find that people disagree on in your class?

Absolute or Relative morality?

Are some things always wrong, no matter what the circumstances?

Some say that there are **absolute moral standards**. These are rules that never change, regardless of the circumstances. For example, we might say '**It is always wrong to kill**'.

Others argue that moral standards are **relative**. This means that we must consider a person's circumstances and reasons for their actions before a judgement about right and wrong can be made. For example, we might say '**It is sometimes acceptable to kill in defending someone else.**'

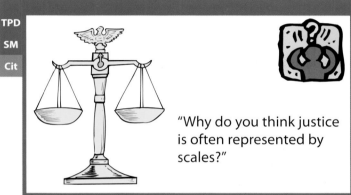

TPD
SM
Cit

"Why do you think justice is often represented by scales?"

The eighth of **the Ten Commandments** says:

'Do not steal' (**Deuteronomy 5:19**)

The laws of our country enforce this rule by sending thieves to jail. However, what if a homeless person is dying of hunger, and they steal some fruit from a market stall in order to stay alive? Is stealing wrong in this situation?

Read this story from **Joshua 2:1-7**.

Here, two Israelite spies working for God are driven into hiding in the city of Jericho. They take refuge in the house of a woman named Rahab. When soldiers come looking for the spies, the story takes an interesting turn:

'The king of Jericho was told, 'Look! Some of the Israelites have come here tonight to spy out the land.'

So the king of Jericho sent this message to Rahab: 'Bring out the men who came to you and entered your house, because they have come to spy out the whole land.' But the woman had taken the two men and hidden them. She said, 'Yes, the men came to me, but I did not know where they had come from. At dusk, when it was time to close the city gate, the men left. I don't know which way they went. Go after them quickly. You may catch up with them.' (But she had taken them up to the roof and hidden them under the stalks of flax she had laid out on the roof.) So the men set out in pursuit of the spies on the road that leads to the fords of the Jordan, and as soon as the pursuers had gone out, the gate was shut.'

Com TPD PD

The ninth of the Ten Commandments instructs us not to tell lies:

'You shall not give false testimony against your neighbour'

(**Deuteronomy 5:20**)

In the story, Rahab tells a lie to protect the Israelites. Is it possible to defend her actions?

Com Cit PD

Take a class vote to see how many believe in **absolute** moral standards and how many believe in **relative** moral standards.

Allow three people from each side of the debate to argue their side and try to convince the rest of the class.

Take a second vote.

Has anyone changed their view? If so, why?

Com BC TPD

In The Dock

Read each of the following case studies and follow the instructions.

1

Mrs Smith is 76

She lives alone but is a bit forgetful and confused at times. She is out shopping when she meets Lily, one of her friends, and they begin to chat. Being a bit absent-minded, Mrs Smith puts the packet of sweets she had chosen for her grandson into her pocket without paying for it. The security guard sees her and Mrs Smith is brought to the manager's office.

2

Lucy Wilson is 16

She competes with her friend Amy to have the most up-to-date, fashionable clothes. On a shopping trip with her mum Lucy sees a gorgeous pair of jeans that cost £120, but her mum says they are too expensive. Back in the changing room Lucy notices that there is no security tag on the jeans. She quickly folds them up and puts them into the bottom of her bag. Lucy and her mum leave the shop undetected.

3

Yan Taleek is 12

He lives in a house made from corrugated iron sheets and old wooden boards. His father died from AIDS three years ago and his mum is very sick. His nine brothers and sisters depend on him for food, but his job as a shoe shiner brings in very little money even though he works long hours. Their home is near a wealthy farm estate with many fruit trees. After dark, Yan climbs the fence, fills his backpack with fruit and hurries home to his family. They will not go to bed hungry tonight.

It is up to you to decide whether Mrs Smith, Lucy and Yan are guilty of theft. Will they be **punished** or will they be **pardoned**?

In groups of **four** you are going to write and perform a roleplay based on each scenario. Each of the characters will tell their story and be questioned about their actions.

- One person will play the lawyer who questions the different characters.

- Three people will play the characters in each story:
    - Mrs Smith, Lily, the security guard.
    - Lucy Wilson, Amy, Lucy's mum.
    - Yan Taleek, Yan's mum, the orchard owner.

At the end of each roleplay the whole class will be the jury, deciding if each person is guilty or not guilty.

A Moral Code

Where do we get our ideas of right and wrong, good and bad? Some people think that we learn these from our family. Others say that people naturally know the difference between right and wrong. Our friends can also influence what we think about certain issues.

In school you may have a set of rules or a **code of conduct** that outlines the values that each pupil is expected to have. This lets you know what kind of behaviour is acceptable and what kind of behaviour is unacceptable. In most areas of work and life there are codes of conduct which people are expected to keep.

MI BC SM

Read the list of the Ten Commandments in **Deuteronomy 5:6-21**.

Make a poster illustrating this famous code of conduct. Include a picture to describe each one.

Com MI BC TPD SM

If you ran the school which of your school rules would you change? Which rules would stay the same? What new rules would you add?

Make a list of your new set of school rules.

Present your list to the class. Be prepared to explain the reasons for your decisions.

In **Matthew 22:37-39**, Jesus summed up the Ten Commandments in two sentences when he said:

'Love the Lord your God with all your heart, with all your soul and with all your mind.'

'Love your neighbour as you love yourself.'

Com TPD

If everyone in the world today lived by this moral code, would it help them to make decisions about right and wrong?

How do you think our world would change if this became part of everyone's moral code of conduct?

Many Christians base their decisions about right and wrong on the Ten Commandments. This list of ten rules form part of a Christian's moral code and helps them to govern their behaviour.

In **Matthew 7:12**, we read that Jesus teaches;

'Do to others what you would have them do to you'.

In other words, you should treat people in the way that you would want to be treated.

Jesus' statement has become known as the **Golden Rule**, and it is perhaps the simplest guide to moral decision making.

| TPD SM | Why do you think that Jesus teaching has been labelled the Golden Rule? |

Christianity is not the only religion to encourage this attitude. Many of the world's religions have a very similar principle in their teaching.

Hindu:

'The true rule is to guard and do by the things of others as you do by your own'.

Muslim:

'Let none of you treat your brothers in a way he himself would dislike to be treated.'

Jewish:

'What is hateful to you, do not do to anyone else.'

Buddhist:

'One should seek for others the happiness one desires for oneself.'

| MI BC WO | If you don't have one already, create and illustrate a code of conduct for good behaviour in your classroom. |

Conscience

Have you ever noticed that you may get an uneasy feeling inside you when you do or say something wrong? This is called your **conscience**: it's the voice inside you which warns you when you are about to do something you shouldn't do.

Many Christians believe that the conscience is one of the ways that God speaks to people.

| SM | Think of an occasion when you acted in a way that you knew was wrong. Answer the following questions:
1 How did you feel afterwards?
2 Was anybody affected by your behaviour?
3 Did you get away with it or were you caught?
4 If you had to face the same situation again, would you act differently? |

Sometimes people know the right decision to make but for one reason or another they do not make it. The Apostle Paul said:

'I do not understand what I do. For what I want to do I do not do, but what I hate I do.'

(Romans 7:15)

We often do things that we realise are wrong but we can't quite explain why we did them. Even though we know we will disappoint our parents, teachers or even ourselves, we still find that we say and do things that we should not do.

The conscience has been described as 'like a triangle inside your body'. When you do things you know are wrong, the triangle jumps around and the corners prick you. The more wrong you do, the more the triangle moves. Eventually, the corners wear off and you can no longer feel it pricking you. If we choose, we can train ourselves to ignore our conscience.

Com TPD PD

Take a few moments to discuss this statement as a class.

1 Do you agree with it?

2 Do you think it is true in all cases?

BC SM

Make a poster illustrating the phrase 'garbage in, garbage out'. You can use your own drawings or cut out pictures from magazines and newspapers.

Com TPD PD

Discuss the following questions as a class:

1 Do you think description of the conscience as a triangle is a good one?

2 Do you think everybody has a conscience?
   • If they do, why do some people commit awful crimes?
   • Do some people simply choose to ignore their conscience?

Research suggests that a typical teenager spends over **18 hours a week** watching television, so it is only natural that what they watch has an influence upon how they view the world.

Garbage In, Garbage Out

Many people say that our morals are affected by the television programmes, films and music we watch and listen to. For example, if we watch a lot of films with swearing in them, we may be more likely to use bad language. Some people have suggested that those who play violent video games might commit violent acts in real life.

The term '**garbage in, garbage out**' is normally used by those who work with computers, but it has been adopted by some people to describe the idea that:

'What we take in through our eyes and our ears will eventually come out through our mouths'.

TPD PD

How much do you think **television** influences your views on what is right and wrong?

Com TPD SM WO Cit PD

Think about the following statement:

'Television is to blame for the amount of violence and bad behaviour in society today.'

Do you agree or disagree?

Have a class debate on the statement.

Each pupil should have three tokens. Every time you speak, you must spend one token. Try to use all your tokens.

Finally, take a class vote on the statement.

Com
BC
TPD

Think of a television programme which you watch regularly. In groups, answer the following questions:

1 How often is this programme on television?
2 What is it about?
3 Why do you like it?
4 Who are your favourite characters?

In your groups, choose one of these programmes and pick out a few characters from the show. Invent a story for the characters involving an accident, social problem or crisis. Write and perform two roleplays showing what happens when:

1 The characters ignore the principle of 'Love your neighbour'.

2 The characters follow the principle of 'Love your neighbour'.

When all groups are finished performing the class will have time to discuss their feelings, reactions and opinions.

Coping with the Challenges of Adolescence

The stage of development between childhood and adulthood is called **adolescence**. During this time, young people develop a great deal, both physically and emotionally.

The change from being a child to being an adult is called **puberty**.

During puberty the pituitary gland in the brain releases hormones into the body. These hormones are responsible for the rapid physical development that teenagers go through as well as the emotional changes that many experience.

Adolescence can be a confusing and difficult time when teenagers have to deal with a great deal of change. Parents and teachers may expect more from them as they are now thought to be on the road to adulthood.

Desire For Independence

When a baby is born it is completely **dependent** on its parents to care for it. It needs adults to make sure:

- It has enough to eat and drink.
- Its clothes and nappies are changed.
- It is kept warm.
- It is washed and dried.

Without an adult to care for it, a baby will quickly fall ill or even die from starvation or neglect.

As a child gets older and begins to move through primary school she will develop physically and mentally. She will become more **independent** and rely less on adults to do things for her. She will still depend on her parents for many things but will be able to make more decisions for herself and take on more responsibility.

MI TPD SM PD	Draw **two columns** and label them as indicated below. Fill in this table in as much detail as possible.

Things a primary school child can do independently	Things a primary school child relies on their parents for

Teenagers are caught somewhere between dependence and independence.

Parents have to learn to loosen their control over their children, whilst teenagers must learn to cope responsibly with their own decision making. Problems may occur when parents find it difficult to let go. Also, teenagers often want more independence than their parents think they can handle.

MI TPD SM PD	Draw **two columns** and label them as indicated below. Fill in this table in as much detail as possible.

Things a teenager can do independently	Things a teenager relies on their parents for

Parent-Child Conflict

All children argue with their parents from time to time. Your parents no doubt fought with their parents when they were young. In fact, they probably clashed over the very same things that cause problems between you and your parents.

This is only natural. As young people enter their teens they start to want more responsibility and independence. However, their parents might be reluctant to allow this because they are concerned for their children's safety and well-being.

Naturally, this leads to disagreements. The children are annoyed that their parents are spoiling their fun, while the parents are annoyed that their children do not realise that they are doing it for their own protection.

Com
PD

It should not be too surprising to discover that many of your classmates fight about the exact same things with their parents.

Pupils should stand in the centre of the classroom. One end of the room will be the **'Mega Strife'** area while the opposite end of the classroom is the **'No Sweat'** area.

Your teacher will read out a list of issues that might cause conflict between children and their parents.
- If the issue can be a source of arguments for you and your parents, move to the **Mega Strife** area.
- If you never fight about this issue, then move to the **No Sweat** area.

After a subject has been called out and pupils have moved to the appropriate area, the teacher will ask you:
- **Why** does this issue cause problems?
- **How** does the argument normally start?
- **What** can you do to prevent it?

Here is the list of potential causes of tension and conflict. You can add your own ideas if you wish:

- The time you come home in the evening
- The amount of time spent on homework
- Choice of clothes
- Phone bill
- How you spend your money
- Going to church
- Choice of music
- Doing well in school or in exams
- Friends
- Doing household chores
- Amount of time you spend on the computer
- Boyfriends / girlfriends
- The way your bedroom is decorated
- Food you eat or don't eat

Arguments are a normal part of growing up, but this does not mean that you should treat your parents disrespectfully. The fifth of the Ten Commandments teaches:

> 'Honour your father and your mother, as the Lord your God has commanded you, so that you may live long and that it way go well with you in the land the Lord your God is giving you.'
>
> **(Deuteronomy 5:16)**

Another word for honour is 'respect'. This means children should respect their parents, even if they don't always agree with them. We should be grateful for the parents who raised us, fed us, clothed us and put a roof over our heads.

Com **TPD** **WO** **PD**

In pairs, discuss:

Do you think there is a difference between obeying our parents and honouring them?

MI **BC**

In **Luke 2:41-50**, we learn about a time when the young Jesus acted in a way that upset his parents. Read the passage and then answer the following questions:

1 How long was Jesus missing for?

2 What does Jesus' mother say to him when they finally find him?

3 Has anyone ever said that to you?

4 Are you surprised that Jesus' actions upset his parents?

Imagine you are Mary or Joseph. Write a letter to a friend back home in Nazareth giving an account of what happened. You might want to talk about:

- How you felt when you discovered that Jesus was missing.
- How you felt when you finally found him.
- If you understood his explanation or found it confusing or upsetting.
- Your concerns for the future.

Anger

Anger can be a very dangerous, negative emotion. Have you ever found that when you start to get angry it's quite often difficult to calm down? Have you ever said something in anger which you regretted later?

ICT **MI** **SM**

Anger is said to be one of the **Seven Deadly Sins**. Go online or visit a library. See if you can find out anything about the Seven Deadly Sins. Do you know what they are or where they came from?

BC **TPD** **SM**

What is anger? How would you define it? Copy and complete the following sentences:

1 A colour I would associate with anger is...

This is because...

2 An object I would associate with anger is...

This is because...

3 An animal I would associate with anger is...

This is because...

4 A place I would associated with anger is...

This is because...

Anger can have very serious consequences. When people are angry, they can stop thinking about their actions and end up making foolish decisions. For example, many crimes are committed when a person is angry. It only takes a moment for them to make a mistake which they will regret forever.

How many times have you seen headlines such as these in a newspaper?

FEMALE DRIVER BECOMES ANOTHER VICTIM OF ROAD RAGE

MAN NEEDS 50 STITCHES AFTER UNPROVOKED ATTACK

TOWN CENTRE VANDALISED BY DRUNKEN MOB

MI
WO

Working in pairs, look through a newspaper for articles describing incidents or events that were the result of anger.

Are you shocked by how many of these incidents are mentioned in a daily newspaper?

What Do the World Faiths Say About Anger?

CHRISTIANITY

There are plenty of instances in the Bible when the reader is taught not to get angry:

'Get rid of all bitterness, rage and anger, brawling and slander, along with every form of malice.'

(Ephesians 4:31)

'A fool gives full vent to his anger, but a wise man keeps himself under control.'

(Proverbs 29:11)

'In your anger do not sin. Do not let the sun go down while you are still angry, and do not give the devil a foothold.'

(Ephesians 4:26-27)

'You have heard it said to the people long ago, 'Do not murder, and anyone who murders will be subject to judgement.' But I tell you that anyone who his angry with his brother will be subject to judgement.'

(Matthew 5:21-22)

MI
TPD
SM

Re-read Matthew 5:21-22 and answer the following questions:

1 What do the words 'brawling', 'slander' and 'malice' mean? Look them up in the dictionary if don't know.

2 What does it mean to 'not let the sun go down while you are still angry'?

3 Do you think Jesus is teaching that being angry with someone was just as bad as murdering them?

BUDDHISM

'If a person comes to create a disturbance, you should hold your peace. You must resist becoming angry with him; then he who has come to curse you will merely harm himself.'

(Sutra of Forty-two Sections, 6)

Com
MI
TPD
SM

Explain the advice that this passage gives in your own words.

HINDUISM

'There are three gates to self-destructive hell: lust, anger and greed.'

(Bhagavad Gita 16:21)

Re-read this verse carefully and then answer the following questions:

1 What do you think these words mean? Why would 'lust, anger and greed' lead to hell?

2 Do you agree with the idea expressed in this verse?

Try writing your own wise saying about anger and self-control.

Discuss the following questions as a class.

1 Think of times when you have **reacted** or **acted**. What was the result in each case?

2 When faced with a tough situation, is it more difficult to **react** or to **act**? Explain your answer.

3 Is taking control of anger something which gets easier as you grow up? Why?

Managing Anger

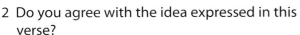

There are two ways in which we can behave when faced with a situation that makes us angry.

React

This means responding in an emotional, uncontrolled way. Fighting fire with fire often makes the situation worse and leads to an **escalation** of the anger. Reacting can result in verbal insults, threats and even violence.

Act

This means taking action that controls the situation. Staying calm and in control allows the person to choose their words and the best course of action carefully.

Workings in groups of **three or four**, invent a situation in which two or more people might be in conflict with one another. Write and perform **two** roleplays with the following outcomes:

1 One in which your characters **react**.

2 One in which your characters **act**.

Which outcome was best? Why?

Imagine that you are an agony aunt (or uncle) for a teenage magazine. What advice would you give to the boy who wrote this letter?

Dear Alex,

I have a problem that a lot of kids my age have too – I can't control my temper. If people at school wind me up I just lose it. They just have to call me a few names or tease me about my schoolbag and I'm gagging for a fight. Sometimes I get cross with the teachers too. I find it really hard not to talk back when they are telling me off. I do my best to hold my tongue, but sometimes I just can't control my anger.

When I go home I really take it out on my family. I say awful things to my mum and sister, things that they don't deserve, but I can't stop myself. Sometimes it feels as if I am watching another person do these things. I realised that I needed help when I threw my Xbox against my bedroom wall after a row with my sister. What can I do? Please help.

Tom

Write a response to Tom offering some practical guidelines to help him deal with his anger.

Substance Abuse

What Is substance abuse?

When most people hear the term **substance abuse** they think of the harmful effects of taking illegal drugs. Substance abuse may refer to the misuse of any of the following substances:

• **Prescription medicines** such as sleeping pills, Valium and Prozac.

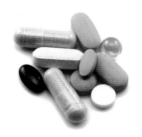

• **Solvents** such as glue, aerosols and paint.

• **Illegal drugs** such as cannabis, cocaine and heroin.

• **Legal drugs** such as alcohol and cigarettes.

Different people have different attitudes to the use of drugs. Some believe them to be harmful and dangerous so they never touch them. Other people only experiment with them once and may never take them again. Others continue to take drugs regularly to the point that they are **addicted** - they cannot do without them.

> Com
> MI
> TPD
> WO
>
> Why do you think people abuse substances? As a class, list as many reasons as you can think of. Write the answers on the board.

Christians and alcohol

Alcohol is probably the drug that you will have heard most about. The subject of drinking and getting drunk continues to be a controversial issue among Christians.

Some Christians do not agree with drinking at all. They argue that alcohol is dangerous and causes many problems in society and that the only way to avoid these problems is through total **abstention**.

This means never drinking alcohol under any circumstances.

Other Christians believe that **moderate** drinking is harmless. They see nothing wrong with having the occasional bottle of wine with a meal or going to the pub to relax in the company of friends.

MI
TPD
SM

What does the Bible have to say?

The Bible makes a number of statements about drinking alcohol. Look up the following verses and fill in the blanks.

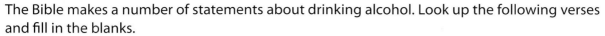

Proverbs 20:1

'Wine is a mocker and beer a brawler; whoever is _____ is _____.'

1 Timothy 5:23

'Stop drinking only water, and use _____ because of your stomach and your _____ .'

Proverbs 23:31-34

'Do not gaze at wine when it is red, when it sparkles in the cup, when it goes down smoothly! In the end it _____ and _____ . Your eyes will _____ and your mind will _____ ___ . You will be like one sleeping on _____ lying on top of the rigging.'

Ephesians 5:18

'Do not get drunk on wine, which leads _____ . Instead, be filled with _____ .'

Psalm 104:15

'Wine that _____ of man, oil to make his face shine, and bread that sustains his heart.'

Proverbs 31:4-5

'It is not for kings, O Lemuel – not for kings to _____ , not for rulers to _____ , lest they drink and _____ and deprive all the oppressed of their rights.'

Some of these verses issue a command to Christians to **refrain from getting drunk**, while others suggest **drinking in moderation**. Can you tell which is which?

Jesus and alcohol

At the time of Jesus, the Jewish religion was exceedingly strict about the use of alcohol. Although drinking was permitted in certain situations, drunkenness was condemned.

In **John 2:1-11**, we read the famous story of Jesus turning water into wine at a wedding in Cana. Look up the passage and read it carefully.

Some bible scholars suggest that Jesus made up to **one hundred and sixty gallons** of wine for the party guests. Some people have asked why Jesus was so keen to produce alcohol. Would he have done this if drinking was viewed as a dangerous pastime?

There are several possible responses to this question:

1 Sanitation at this time was so poor that it was often safer to drink wine than water.

2 It is argued that wine in Biblical times was much weaker than the kind that people drink today.

3 It would have been incredibly embarrassing for the family hosting the wedding to run out of wine. Jesus tried to save the family any humiliation by performing this miracle.

4 Drinking and riding a donkey was much less dangerous than drinking and driving.

TPD Can you think of any other reasons why Jesus turned the water into wine?

**MI
BC
SM**
Read **John 2:1-11** again. Imagine you are a journalist writing for a newspaper in the town of Cana.

Write an article on Jesus' actions at the wedding.

You may want to include interviews with some of the people who were there.

They are curious	
It makes them feel grown up	
Someone offers it to them	
They are lonely	
To forget about their problems	
To take away the pain of an illness	

Drugs

'Drug misuse is a major threat to individuals, families and the wider community, in Northern Ireland as in the rest of the UK and further afield'

(*Misuse of Drugs: Guidance for Schools*, DENI, 1996)

**TPD
Cit
PD**
Are you shocked by this statement? Or are you not really bothered?

The Bible makes many references to drinking alcohol but it does not mention any other kinds of drug taking. The Bible does give important lifestyle guidelines that can be applied to taking drugs.

Christians believe that God wants them to live a life that is pleasing to him. In **Ephesians 4:22**, Paul tells Christians to leave behind their old habits and ways and live a new life:

'You were taught, with regard to your former way of life, to put off your old self, which is being corrupted by its deceitful desires.'

There are three questions a Christian should ask themselves when they are wondering whether or not to take drugs:

How can Christians help addicts?

Many Christians argue that it is wrong to abuse the body and the mind with drugs. At the same time, Christians agree that drug addicts and those with drug-related problems need care and help.

One thing that churches can do is think about the reasons why people take drugs in the first place. Many people assume that those who take drugs are either stupid or careless, but there is much more to it than that. Many different social problems cause people from all areas of life to become addicted.

TPD Copy the table below. For each of the reasons listed, try and think of things the Christian Church could do to prevent people from becoming addicted.

Why people take drugs	What could the Church do?
They like the feeling that alcohol and drugs give them	
They are bored	
They are pressurised by friends	

1 How will a drug affect my body?

Drugs can be incredibly harmful to the human body. They can weaken your mind, damage your health and greatly affect your emotions. It's important to look after one's personal health and fitness. Perhaps a question everybody should ask themselves is 'will this substance damage my body?'

> Read **Daniel 1**. In this chapter, Daniel chooses not to eat the food or drink the wine given to him.
>
> What can we learn about Daniel's attitude in this chapter?

2 Will it affect my Christian faith?

Christians are also concerned with how certain actions will affect their faith. The Bible speaks of God's desire to fill his followers with the Holy Spirit (**Ephesians 5:18**). For this to happen, a Christian should be clear-minded and have control over their behaviour, which would mean that they should not take drugs. They affect a person's mind by slowing it down, speeding it up or causing confusion.

3 How will taking a drug affect others?

The Bible talks about the importance of setting an example for others. Though we might not be able to see it, our actions influence those around us. Therefore, we should be careful about our behaviour and not act in a way that causes other people to sin (**1 Corinthians 8:13**). The Apostle Paul says;

> 'Whatever you do, whether you eat or drink, do it all for God's glory'
>
> **(1 Corinthians 10:31)**

As a Christian it is important to examine the possible effect of your behaviour on others.

| Com |
| BC |
| Cit |
| PD |

 Why not write, perform or even film your own television advertisement or short documentary warning of the dangers of taking drugs?

Smoking

Everyone knows that smoking is not good for a healthy body. While you are young you may not think about the effects that smoking can have on your body in the long term, but it leads to discoloured teeth and fingers, it affects your breathing, and it can cause many serious diseases.

By law, each packet of cigarettes must carry a warning which clearly states that smoking does damage to a person's health.

More than 90% of all lung cancer victims are smokers, and studies have also shown that smokers have more than three times as many heart attacks as non-smokers.

In the Bible, the apostle Paul writes;

> 'Don't you know that you yourselves are God's temple and that God's spirit lives in you! If anyone destroys God's temple, God will destroy him; for God's temple is sacred, and you are that temple.'
>
> **(I Corinthians 3:16-17)**

Obviously, Christians need to think very carefully about something as dangerous to your health as smoking.

| TPD |
| SM |

The dangers of smoking are well known. All Cigarette packets carry serious health warnings. Why do you think people continue to smoke?

In **Romans 14:21** and **15:1-2** Christians are taught not to offend others. Some people do not notice smoking, but most people do not like the habit and others are greatly offended by it. It is important to be considerate and thoughtful.

Research has shown that repeatedly breathing in second hand smoke, known as **passive smoking**, can cause severe health problems for the non-smoker. If someone's body is damaged because they are a smoker, then it is the result of their own actions. They have made a choice to smoke. People whose bodies are damaged by passive smoking have not been allowed to make that choice.

Smoking wastes time and money, and Christians are told to use their money wisely. (**Matthew 25:14-30**).

Spending a lot of money on cigarettes can mean that children and other adults are deprived of the more important things that they need, such as food and clothing, and even homes. Millions of pounds are spent every year buying tobacco. In the Old Testament, God says;

'Why spend money on what is not bread, and your labour on what does not satisfy? Listen, listen to me, and eat what is good, and your soul will delight in the richest of fare.'

(**Isaiah 55:2**)

ICT	
MI	Design a poster outlining the dangers of smoking.
BC	Use the internet or library to research details and statistics about smoking.
SM	Your poster should contain text and images. Try to make your poster appeal to people the same age as you.

A Personal Example

This is a photograph of my Dad taken in 1970. He is pictured here with my younger brother who is now 38 years old. It appeared in our local newspaper which ran an article on attitudes towards smoking. In the interview he said, 'I've smoked since I was eight years old and it never did me any harm!'

He died in 1999 of lung cancer, aged 71. He didn't live to see my children. I hope this makes you think twice about smoking.

- Juliana Gilbride

Further Information

Alcohol Concern

(information about alcohol issues)

020 7928 7377 **www.alcoholconcern.org.uk**

Institute of Alcohol Studies

(information and statistics about alcohol issues)

020 7222 4001 **www.ias.org.uk**

DrugScope

(information about drugs and drug issues)

020 7928 1211 **www.drugscope.org.uk**

European Monitoring Centre for Drugs and Drug Addiction

(information about European drug issues)

www.emcdda.eu.int

FRANK

(Government run drugs information and helpline)

0800 77 66 00 **www.talktofrank.com**

Government Drugs website

www.drugs.gov.uk

MI
TPD
SM

Fact Or Opinion?

Look at the list of statements below. Decide which are **fact** and which are **opinion**.

- 'Drugs harm your health.'
- 'Smoking is a bad habit.'
- 'More than 90% of lung cancer victims are smokers'
- 'Drinking alcohol is just as bad as taking cocaine.'
- 'Smoking increases the risk of heart attacks and lung cancer.'
- 'It is illegal to drive under the influence of alcohol.'
- 'Smoking makes you look grown up.'
- '66% of smokers say they want to give up.'
- Compared to other drugs, cannabis isn't that bad.

How did you decide which was fact and which was opinion?

Are there any opinions that you disagreed with?

Are there any facts that you could add to the list?

Peers

The word **peers** refers to the group of people who are the same age as you: those in your class or place of work.

The term **peer group** refers to your group of friends.

You will have lots of peers because you go to school. Your group of friends is not limited to the classroom and may also include family, those who go to your church or a club, or those who go to other schools.

As well as having different friends, there are different types of friendship:

- Sometimes we have friends with whom we get along with very well, but we would not tell them our most personal secrets.

- Other friendships are deeper – we feel that we can share anything with them.

- Some of our friends are younger than us and some are older. You may have friends that you have known since playgroup or you may have changed all your friends since moving to secondary school.

MI
BC
SM

What types of friendships do you have?

Make a list of your friends and try to group them into categories, for example: Church friends; school friends; friends through sport; older friends etc.

Colour code each group.

Key

○ Church friends
● School friends
● Sport friends
○ Older friends

○● James
● Benjamin
○● Emily
●● Joshua
●○ Hanna

Peer Pressure

Our friends influence our decisions. You will notice that groups of friends often like the same music or television programmes or have the same hobbies. The more they are together, the more they become alike. Some groups of friends even dress like each other.

The main reason for this is **peer pressure** - the feeling that you ought to change your behaviour to match that of your peers.

It is perfectly natural to want to 'fit in' with our group of friends, but peer pressure becomes dangerous whenever people feel pressured into doing something they do not want to do.

For example, people may try to convince you to stay out later than your parents allow. They may tell you that is not important to keep to you parents' wishes. By going along with the crowd you could cause your parents to worry that something bad had happened to you.

Many teenagers feel pressured into smoking or drinking alcohol, particularly if some of their friends do it. Not only are these activities illegal until a person is 18 years of age, but research has shown that underage drinking has an effect on a person's health. The effects of smoking are well known, and yet some still feel pressured into doing it.

TPD SM PD

Mostly, we think of peer pressure as something that happens **to us**, but can you think of a time when you might have put pressure on a friend to do something they didn't want to do?

WHY GIVE IN TO PEER PRESSURE?

The desire to 'fit in' is particularly strong in teenagers. People want to be liked, to feel accepted, to impress others.

Negative behaviour is made to seem normal when we are told that 'everybody's doing it'. People feel that they we will be left out unless they take part.

We should not underestimate the strength of peer pressure to influence our decisions.

DEALING WITH PEER PRESSURE

It is tough to be the only person who says 'no'. Our friends are often the hardest people to stand up to. There are a number of responses to negative peer pressure:

- Walk away.
- Having another friend who is willing to say 'no' takes a lot of the power out of peer pressure.
- Have other friends. If people are pressuring you to do something you don't want to, then they're not being very good friends.
- Talk to someone. If the pressure is hard to handle, you can talk to someone you trust, such as a parent or teacher.

MI BC WO

In **pairs**, make a poster showing some of the ways teenagers feel pressured by their peers and suggesting some ways to deal with peer pressure.

Peer pressure can also have a positive effect. If someone is taking part in negative behaviour such as smoking or being nasty toward others, a group of strong friends who refuse to join in can help them improve their behaviour.

TPD SM

You may have heard the phrase "One bad apple spoils the whole barrel'

- What does this phrase mean?

- Do you agree with it?

You've probably heard your parents or teachers tell you to 'choose your friends wisely'. We find the same advice in the Bible, in **1 Corinthians 15:33**:

'Do not be misled: 'Bad company corrupts good character."

We should not underestimate the effect that our friends have on our behaviour. Our choice of friends shapes the people we will be in the future.

Friends of Jesus

Choosing friends does not always mean choosing the people who are most popular, or most like us. Jesus was friends with all sorts of people, including those who were ignored by the rest of society. He was happy to befriend poor people, street beggars, prostitutes and lepers.

Many people were shocked at some of the people with whom Jesus spent his time. They felt that these people were not suitable companions for a religious teacher.

One man who became a friend of Jesus was Zacchaeus, a chief tax collector. The Jewish people despised and rejected tax collectors for several reasons:

- They worked for the enemy, the Romans.
- The coins they handled were engraved with images of the Roman gods.
- They were greedy and cheated people out of their money.
- They were often sneaky and accepted bribes.

ZACCHAEUS THE TAX COLLECTOR

'Jesus entered Jericho and was passing through. A man was there by the name of Zacchaeus; he was a chief tax collector and was wealthy. He wanted to see who Jesus was but being a short man he could not, because of the crowd. So he ran ahead and climbed a sycamore-fig tree to see him, since Jesus was coming that way.

When Jesus reached the spot, he looked up and said to him, 'Zacchaeus, come down immediately. I must stay at your house today.' So he came down at once and welcomed him gladly.

All the people saw this and began to mutter, 'He has gone to be the guest of a 'sinner'.

But Zacchaeus stood up and said to the Lord, 'Look, Lord! Here and now I give half of my possessions to the poor, and if I have cheated anybody out of anything, I will pay back four times the amount."

(Luke 19:1- 8)

You will notice that the crowd reacted with shock and disgust when Jesus approached Zacchaeus. He did not act as the crowd expected him to but took time to speak with Zacchaeus and even stayed as a guest in his house.

MI
TPD
SM

Read **Luke 19:1-8** and answer the following questions:

1 Why do you think Jesus spoke with Zacchaeus when nobody else did?

2 How did the other people describe Zacchaeus? Why do you think they did this?

3 What effect did Jesus's actions have on Zacchaeus?

4 Can you think of an example of an unpopular person who would be hard to talk to? For example, think of a character from a film or television programme you have watched or from a book you have read. Write a description of how you think Jesus would deal with this person.

BC
SM

Imagine that you are Zacchaeus. Write a detailed diary entry describing the day you met Jesus.

As well as befriending outcasts in society, Jesus chose twelve men to be his disciples. These were the people Jesus was closest to during his ministry. Jesus did not just pick men that would immediately meet society's approval. For example, Simon was a Zealot who hated the Romans, Matthew had been a tax collector, and Peter had a fierce temper!

Jesus spent a great deal of time with his disciples, teaching them how to behave towards each other and towards other people. He explained that true friendship means putting the other person first:

'Greater love has no one than this, that he lay down his life for his friends.'

(**John 15:13**)

TPD SM
Apart from Jesus, can you think of an example from history, books or films of someone who gave up their life for their friends?

TPD SM
Make a list of ways that you might put others before yourself.

Why is this sometimes difficult to do?

Trust

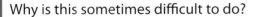

Trust is an important part of every friendship. Some friends we will trust very closely. It is good to have someone we can share our thoughts and

feelings with, knowing that they will not be telling anyone else about it.

Breaking trust destroys friendship very quickly, and being betrayed by a friend is one of the most hurtful things that can happen to anyone. Being trustworthy is a vital part of being a good friend.

MI TPS WO
In **threes**, copy the table below and fill the columns with examples.

What trust is...	What trust is not...
Keeping a secret	Gossiping

TPD SM PD
Are you trustworthy? Are you the kind of person people can tell their secrets to? What is the biggest thing you have ever been trusted with?

Trust also means that we refuse to listen to gossip and rumours about a particular person. We can decide for ourselves whether or not they are a good friend.

PAUL

In the New Testament, many of Jesus' first followers were **persecuted**. One of the worst persecutors of the early church was a Pharisee named **Saul** (not to be confused with King Saul from the Old Testament). He was on his way to Damascus to destroy the Christian fellowship there when he had a vision of Jesus (**Acts 9:1-19**). He was so affected by this vision that he became a Christian.

This caused a problem. How could the others trust him? After all, he was a dangerous man who had been responsible for the deaths of many of their friends.

Everyone was very wary of Saul, but now he was a Christian and therefore one of them.

Surely they had to befriend him, welcome him into their community and show him love as Jesus had told them to do.

Jesus taught his followers to forgive their enemies. They must have found it difficult to trust Saul, but they did forgive him and welcomed him. Afterwards, **Saul changed his name to Paul** and became one of the most important members of the early Christian Church.

The story of Saul's conversion shows the importance of giving people a second chance, even if they don't deserve it.

MI
TPD
SM

1 Why did the early Christians find it difficult to trust Saul when he became a Christian?

2 Do you think that Saul deserved a second chance? Give reasons for your answer.

3 What does Jesus teach about forgiveness?

4 Can you think of a situation where it would be difficult to forgive a friend?

5 What advice would you give in that situation?

Disagreements

Mostly, friendships provide a happy and positive experience for us, but sometimes even the closest of friends disagree and argue. This is normal.

Friends can disagree over many issues, big and small, and sometimes disagreements can cause friends to fall out. This may only last for a few hours or a few days, but sometimes a broken friendship is never mended and people go their separate ways.

You can probably think of people that you were once very friendly with but perhaps because of some disagreement you don't hang around with them any more.

There are even times in the Bible when God's people disagreed with each other. In the New Testament, Paul and Peter have a disagreement about how Christians should behave. In **Galatians 2:11**, Paul explains how he confronted Peter:

'I opposed him to his face, because he was clearly in the wrong.'

Paul believed that sometimes friends have to tell each other the truth about something they have done or something about their character that they do not agree with. The same rule applies to our friendships nowadays. We can be friends with someone but we don't have to agree with them about everything.

TPD
SM
PD

1 Think of a time you had a disagreement with a friend. How did it make you feel?

2 How important do you think honesty is in a friendship?

3 Do you think there are ever times when it is right not to be honest?

4 What can we learn from the relationship between Peter and Paul?

Fellowship

Christian friendship is about sharing the same faith. This is sometimes called 'fellowship'. For Christians, simply 'believing' things is not enough, they have to put their faith into action. In friendships this means being trustworthy, putting the other person first, and forgiving easily, just as Jesus taught.

Christians don't always believe exactly the same things, but they can still be in fellowship together like Peter and Paul.

A church family having a meal together in the church hall.

In Paul's Letter to the Ephesians he gives advice that is important for friendship:

'If you become angry, do not let your anger lead you into sin, and do not stay angry all day.' (**Ephesians 4:26**)

This means that if you argue with a friend it is best to try to sort out the problem as quickly as possible.

TPD SM
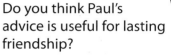
If you are angry with a friend how might your anger 'lead you into sin'?

Do you think Paul's advice is useful for lasting friendship?

How can it apply to other relationships as well?

MI TPD SM PD

The following story describes a disagreement between two friends. Read the story and answer the questions that follow:

Sarah and Becky had been inseparable since they had started secondary school. They went to computer club together and Scripture Union after school. When they weren't in school, they were forever texting and phoning each other.

Sarah went to bed early on Friday night. She was nearly asleep when her phoned beeped. It was a message from Becky. 'Good luck for tomorrow!' it read. Sarah smiled. She was taking part in a gymnastics competition. I'll reply in the morning, she thought, and went to sleep.

'Sarah! Sarah! It's time to get up,' Mum shouted up the stairs. Sarah groaned. She felt awful. It must be the flu... even her bones ached. It was Saturday!

She had to go to the competition. Her gym instructor was expecting her, and everyone in school would ask how she had got on, so she dragged herself out of bed.

The competition did not go well. 'I was awful. But you know, Mum, I don't even care. I just feel so sick! I've been really stupid going today. All I want to do is go to bed.'

When they got home Sarah jumped into bed with a hot water bottle. Within minutes she was nearly asleep. Her phoned beeped. 'There's a message on your phone,' said Mum.

'No, it's the battery dying. I forgot to charge it.'

Sarah was dreaming. Her dog Buster was in the gymnastics competition and had just won a gold medal. Then a fire bell went off and everyone started to panic... 'Sarah', a voice was calling, 'Sarah!'

Sarah woke up. Mum was in her bedroom holding the phone. 'Oh good, you're awake, love. It's Sunday. Nearly seven. You've slept all day. It's Becky on the phone.'

'What's the problem, Sarah? There's obviously a problem!' Becky growled. She sounded different, really aggressive. 'There's obviously some problem between us. Are you fed up with me? You usually text me three times a day and I haven't heard a word since Friday. What have I done?'

'No, no. Becky, what are you saying? I've... I've had the competition and I've been really, really sick.'

'Not that sick that you could go to the competition!' Becky snipped.

'I haven't been avoiding you. Anyway, I haven't heard from you either.'

'Now you're really twisting things. I sent you a good luck message on Friday night and you didn't even reply. You need to have a good look at yourself.' Becky slammed down the phone.

Sarah cried and cried. This vicious attack seemed to have come out of nowhere. She couldn't believe how nasty Becky had been. Sure, she had only known her for a few months but she had thought she was a real friend.

'She's probably right, mum.' Sarah cried. 'I was texting her at least three times a day, but I've been so busy and sick this weekend that I forgot.'

'Friends don't count how many times someone has been in touch with them or who phoned last. A real friend would understand that you had your reasons for not being in touch.'

'I know, Mum but Becky and I are Christians. She's supposed to be different.'

'No one is perfect, dear. Anyway, it's not up to us to judge. You know that. I think you should give Becky some space for a while and concentrate on getting better.'

'Okay. I'll just leave things until I see Becky again at school. But to be honest I don't know what to say when I see her again.'

Think carefully about the story and answer the following questions in your classwork books:

1 What sort of friendship do Becky and Sarah have?

2 Do you think Becky is being unreasonable? Give reasons for your answer.

3 How do you think Sarah should react to Becky when she sees her in school?

4 In pairs, look at the following verses, and suggest what advice an older Christian might give to Sarah and Becky.

- Ephesians 4:26
- Proverbs 17:17
- Proverbs 18:24
- Ecclesiastes 4:9

Like Sarah in the story, you may have had the experience of being hurt by someone. Maybe you do not want to give that particular person a second chance, or maybe you do not want to get too close to anybody again.

However, human beings need close friendships, especially as they start to get older. It is important to have people with whom you can share experiences and who will be there for you in difficult times. Having good friends helps us to become confident and to grow into mature adults.

Forgiveness

If someone does something wrong against us we can feel hurt and angry. Some people feel they should take revenge. If someone gets hit, they hit back. If someone has a trick played on them, they think up an even nastier trick to play.

Forgiveness is when we no longer hold a person's wrongs against them. We do not bear a grudge, and we do not take revenge.

For Christians forgiveness is a way of life. They feel that, as God has forgiven them for their wrongdoing, so they should forgive everyone who wrongs them. **Colossians 3:13** gives specific instructions to Christians who feel that they have been wronged by each other:

> 'Bear with each other and forgive whatever grievances you may have against one another. Forgive as the Lord forgave you.'

Sometimes it is necessary to put our differences behind us for the sake of friendship.

MI TPD PD

1 What problems in the world might disappear if people forgave their 'grievances' with each other?

Read **Matthew 6:12-14**.

2 What does it tell Christians about forgiveness?

3 Why might a Christian feel they ought to forgive?

On one occasion, one of Jesus' disciples asked him a question about forgiveness.

> 'Then Peter came to Jesus and asked, 'Lord, how many times shall I forgive my brother when he sins against me? Up to seven times?' Jesus answered, 'I tell you, not seven times, but seventy-seven times.'

(Matthew 18:21-22)

Peter obviously thinks that forgiving someone seven times is a lot, but Jesus challenges him to think bigger. When Jesus says seventy seven, he is not setting an upper limit on how many times we should forgive. He is telling Peter that forgiveness should not have boundaries.

TPD WO PD

In groups, discuss the following question:

How many times do you think you can forgive someone?

How many times should you forgive someone?

Forgiveness is not...

Forgiveness does not mean pretending that a person has not hurt you. Forgiveness means acknowledging the person's mistake, and choosing not to hold it against them.

Forgiveness does not mean being weak or foolish.

If someone who claims to be your friend continually or deliberately hurts you, you can still forgive them, but perhaps it is best to walk away.

TPD SM PD

Apologising

Why do you think is it so hard to apologise, even when we know we did something wrong?

Would you rather have a friend who apologises for their mistakes, or a friend who never admits they are wrong?

David and Jonathan

David and Jonathan are a good example of friendship in the Bible. Their friendship overcomes many difficulties, and they remain friends even under threat of death!

TPD SM PD

What do you think makes a best friend and how do friends prove they are real friends?

You might have learnt about David the shepherd boy in primary school. The most famous story about him is when he killed the giant warrior Goliath with a slingshot. After the battle Saul, the King of Israel, took David into his household where he became friends with Saul's son, Jonathan.

David was very popular with the people. Saul became jealous of David and plotted to kill him. When Jonathan found out what his father was planning he was horrified. He couldn't understand how his father would want to kill his best friend, so he tried to warn David. David and Jonathan made a friendship pact, saying that they would be loyal to each other no matter what happened (**1 Samuel 18:3**).

TPD **SM**	1 Why is it important to be a good friend in difficult circumstances? 2 What qualities should a friend have to be able to cope with stressful times? 3 How do you think Jonathan felt when his father tried to kill David? 4 What words would you use to describe David and Jonathan's friendship?

Saul's jealousy put a strain on his son Jonathan. David had to hide from Saul and he depended on Jonathan for information about possible danger. Jonathan had to choose between respecting his father and being loyal to his friend.

TPD **SM** **PD**	1 Can you think of any situations where someone may have to choose between being loyal to their friends and respecting their own family? 2 David and Jonathan were in a unique situation. Do you think friends should normally put each other before their families?

On one occasion, Saul invites David for a meal, hoping to get the chance to kill him. When Jonathan will not tell his father where David is, he loses his temper:

> 'Saul's anger flared up at Jonathan and he said to him, 'You son of a perverse and rebellious woman! Don't I know that you have sided with the son of Jesse to your own shame and to the shame of the mother who bore you? As long as the son of Jesse lives on this earth, neither you nor your kingdom will be established. Now send and bring him to me, for he must die!'

> 'Why should he be put to death? What has he done?' Jonathan asked his father. But Saul hurled his spear at him to kill him. Then Jonathan knew that his father intended to kill David.

> Jonathan got up from the table in fierce anger; on that second day of the month he did not eat, because he was grieved at his father's shameful treatment of David.'

(**1 Samuel 20: 30-34**)

MI **TPD** **PD**	Read **1 Samuel 20: 30-34.** 1 How do we know that Saul was very angry? 2 What affect do you think getting angry or violent has on those closest to us? 3 Why do you think Jonathan was in such a rage following his father's outburst?

David needed to escape from Saul. He would have to part company with Jonathan. The friends didn't know when they would see each other again.

Some friendships end when one person moves away to live somewhere else. Often people fully intend to keep in touch but their new life takes over and the old friendship fades away. Sometimes people are not allowed to be friends with others because their parents do not approve of them. Whatever the reason, the end of a friendship is often hard to deal with.

TPD
SM
PD
Have you ever put your own success before a friendship?

Is it good to put other people first? Why?

Com
BC
SM
Draw the following speech bubble in your notebook.

Using the example of the story of David, think of two or three sentences to complete the statement.

> A true friendship is one where...

MI
TPD
PD
Read **1 Samuel 20: 41-42**.

1 How difficult would it have been for David and Jonathan to part company?

2 Make a list of emotions they might have felt.

3 For what other reasons do friendships end?

4 If David and Jonathan were alive today, how might they maintain their friendship from a distance?

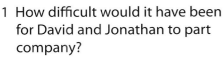

You can read the full story of David and Jonathan in **1 Samuel 18-20**.

Jonathan could have been king after his father, but now David was going to become king. By helping David escape Jonathan showed that his friendship was more important than being king.

Family

Traditionally, a **family** is defined as **a group of people made up of parents and their children, whether living together or not**. In recent years, however, the family unit has changed a great deal.

Families are much smaller than they used to be. A family may not necessarily be made up of a father, mother and a couple of children. For example, some children live with their grandparents or are brought up by a single parent or guardian.

Types of family

Nuclear family

Husband, wife and children.

Extended family

Husband, wife, children, grandparents, aunts, uncles and cousins.

Single parent family

Children brought up by one parent.

Blended family

Families where one or both parents have divorced and remarried. May include children from two families.

Wider family

Families and friends who share the same house.

Single people

Those who are unmarried, widowed or divorced.

Images of the family

Apart from our own family, and the families of our friends and schoolmates, we also see different types of families on television. Some of you may spend a lot of time watching shows which may have an influence on your attitudes and opinions. In some popular TV soap operas families often suffer from divorce, debt, alcoholism and domestic violence.

Some people argue that the more that we see images like this on television, the more we are prepared to view them as acceptable.

Com
TPD
WO
Cit
PD

Discuss with a partner:

Do you think that families on television influence what we think of as 'normal' family life?

Com
WO

In **pairs**, discuss what you were like when you were very young.

• How much can you remember about your early years?

• Do you know any funny stories about yourself as a toddler?

• What is your earliest memory?

> 'I can remember one Sunday before church. My Daddy let my brother and me play in the back garden. It was a lovely day but it had been raining the night before and there was a really big puddle. All I can remember is wondering why Daddy was so cross when he found us sitting in the puddle in our best clothes, splashing each other. This is my earliest memory. I reckon I was about three years old and my brother was two.'

The importance of families

From the moment we are born we are affected by those around us. As babies, we are looked after by our family. They influence the kind of person each of us will become as we grow older and develop mentally and spiritually.

In most cases, families give children their first experience of love and kindness. Through this, young children can learn the importance of loyalty in a very simple way. As we get older we support each other through difficult and trying periods and we also enjoy good times together.

MI
TPD
Cit
PD

All families are different. Each one is important to those who are part of it.

Copy out the following diagram. Can you add any ideas of your own?

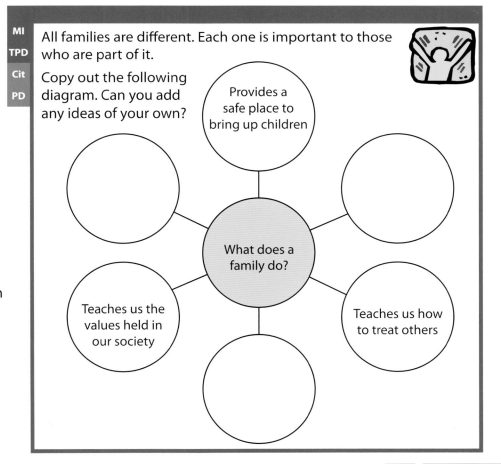

What does a family do?

- Provides a safe place to bring up children
- Teaches us the values held in our society
- Teaches us how to treat others

Spending time with your family

No matter how big or small your family is, it is important to spend time together. This does not mean simply being in the same house but actually talking to each other or taking part in an activity.

Ma MI SM WO

Make a personal list of the activities you do with your family. For example, do you eat a meal together every day? Compare your list with others in your class. As a class make a bar chart to illustrate how people in your class spend time with their families.

Number of pupils (y-axis): 0, 5, 10, 15, 20, 25, 30
Categories (x-axis): Shop, TV, Meals, Church, ?

Christian Families

Many people in Northern Ireland would consider themselves to be Christian. This has an influence upon their family life. They believe that the family is part of God's plan for caring for people. This means caring for their young people by teaching them religious and moral values.

Some Christian churches baptise children. Parents take vows that they will raise their child in the Christian faith. The whole congregation also plays an important part in this ceremony by promising to help the parents. Therefore, the whole Church is seen as being like a family.

ICT MI TPD

See if you can find a copy of a baptism service for infants. Answer the following questions:

1. What are the vows which are made by the parents?
2. Do you think these promises would be difficult to keep?

TPD WO

The following list suggests some of the ways in which parents can keep their Christian vows.

In pairs, talk about each one and why a Christian family might do this.

Can you add any more activities to the list?

- Saying grace before every meal.
- Treating Sunday as a day of rest.
- Praying together as a family.
- Reading the Bible together.
- Going to church together.

Conflict in the Family

Look at the two cartoons below. What do they tell us about parents and teenagers?

'Why did you write in your diary that I'm nosey?'

'Don't worry, dear. I think he's just going through a phase.'

Conflict between parents and their children is common in every family. It doesn't only happen during the teenage years. In fact, many of you will remember disagreements with your parents when you were much younger.

– Mum, give me another biscuit. I've only had one.

– No, Joshua, it'll ruin your dinner. Now go and play in your room.

– Please, Mum. I'm starving. I never get biscuits!

– I said no. You can't have another biscuit now.

You can have one after dinner.

– It's not fair! That's ages away! I'm starving and you don't care!

– Here's the biscuits! Take them! Eat them all! As long as you have your way that's all that matters!

TPD SM PD

Did you ever have a conversation like this when you were younger?

Now that you are a bit older can you understand why Joshua's mum did not want to give him biscuits?

Can you relate this to any present day situations in your own life?

MI TPD SM PD

Causes of conflict

Copy the diagram below. Add your own ideas to show issues that may cause conflict in the family.

Staying out late

Homework · CONFLICT · Chores

Who has the TV remote

Compare your diagram with a partner. Are any of your causes of conflict the same? Do some of these issues cause more serious conflict than others?

TPD PD

Can you think of a time when your parents or guardians were angry with you?

A time when you realised you had pushed them too far?

BC WO PD In groups of **four**, write and perform a role-play based on a situation of conflict between parents and their children.

Rules of the house?

Mum, what is it with all these rules you keep making up? School days are supposed to be the happiest days of my life!

In your case, maybe your primary school days! These are definitely your most moody days so far. You need some rules to rein you in!

Being part of a family normally means being part of a household with its own habits and rules. Parents have the right to decide which rules to introduce in their home. It is a parent's responsibility to make sure their children are safe and well and this involves creating a set of guidelines for maintaining standards of discipline and safety.

Rules can sometimes be a source of conflict in the family, particularly between teenagers and parents. As teenagers begin to think more independently it is only natural that they will have differences of opinion with their parents. It is important to remember that parents almost always have their children's best interests at heart. Also, children need to learn to respect their parents and other guardians and a set of house rules makes this much easier.

TPD SM PD Can you think of a time when you argued with your parents over house rules? How was the argument resolved? If you were in the same situation again what would you do differently?

Rules are important in all areas of life. Drivers and motorcyclists must follow the Highway Code to prevent accidents. Every society has laws to deter criminals and thieves. We need rules whether we like them or not.

Com PD Have a class debate on the statement: **"My house, my rules"**.

TPD SM WO Imagine you have your own house and two small children.

What kind of rules do you need to introduce in order to keep them safe?

Make a list, then share your thoughts as a class.

TPD WO PD Should teenagers be allowed to make rules for their parents? In pairs, make a list of rules you think parents should have to follow. For example;

• Do not make embarrassing jokes in front of my friends.

• Keep out of my room.

WHAT DOES THE BIBLE SAY?

The Bible teaches that family members have duties and responsibilities towards each other. In **Colossians 3:20-21** we read:

> 'Children, always obey your parents, for this pleases the Lord. Fathers, do not aggravate your children, or they will become discouraged.'

(Scripture quotation taken from the Holy Bible, New Living Translation, copyright (c) 1996. Used by permission of Tyndale House Publishers, Inc., Wheaton, Illinois 60189. All rights reserved.)

While parents should keep their children under control, they should not be too hard on them or irritate them. Similarly children should do what their parents tell them.

Families have a duty to care for each family member. In **1 Timothy 5:8** we read:

> 'If anyone does not provide for his relatives, and especially for his immediate family, he has denied the faith and is worse than an unbeliever.'

This shows how important it is to look after each other. This may be especially important to remember when someone is sick, or if you have an older relative such as a grandparent, who requires care.

Honesty

Honesty is very important in family relationships. Jesus told the Parable of the Two Sons to stress the importance of obeying our parents and being honest in what we say to them.

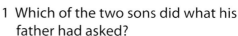

> 'What do you think? There was a man who had two sons. He went to the first and said, 'Son, go and work today in the vineyard.' 'I will not,' he answered, but later he changed his mind and went. Then the father went to the other son and said the same thing. He answered, 'I will, sir,' but he did not go.'

(Matthew 21:28-31)

MI

TPD

Read the passage again carefully and answer the following questions:

1 Which of the two sons did what his father had asked?

2 Do you ever promise to do something and then not bother doing it? Can you give an example?

3 Make a list of all the members of your family and the different jobs they do around the house.
   • Is the work divided equally?
   • Does one person always end up doing the things that others have promised to do?

4 How do your family react when you do a job without being asked?

Loyalty

Most people feel a sense of loyalty to their family. You might find that your brother or sister drives you mad, but if somebody was being nasty to them you would probably want to stick up for them.

Loyalty is a very admirable quality but there are some situations where loyalty isn't straight forward. Sometimes it is important not to hide problems from those outside your family. For example, the entire family may suffer if one of its members is an alcoholic or has another addiction. The family might want to keep the problem hidden but doing this can lead to further, even worse problems.

Sometimes it helps to open up to a family friend or a teacher. Whoever teenagers choose to talk to, it is very important that they do not feel that they are suffering alone.

TPD Read the letter below.

My name's Sarah and I'm fifteen years old.

There have been problems at home for a while now. My Dad has a problem with drugs. At first things weren't too bad but when Dad's addiction started to get worse Mum told me that I had to keep our business private. I haven't had a friend over to the house in years!

Dad is now so badly addicted that he's started to sell all our stuff to pay for drugs. Mum just cries all the time. I'm really worried for my little sister.

I don't feel there's anyone I can talk to. What should I do?

Write a reply giving advice and suggest **three** steps Sarah can take to get help with her problem.

As people grow older their loyalty may change direction. For example, when a person gets married and has children of their own, their relationship with their parents or siblings will take second place to their relationship with their new family. Of course, this does not mean that they stop caring for their first family. It's just that their focus in life has changed.

An example of family loyalty can be seen in the story of Ruth and Naomi. Ruth is married to Naomi's son. She remains loyal to her mother-in-law even after the death of her husband. Ruth's loyalty is shown in **Ruth 1:16-17**.

'But Ruth replied, 'Don't urge me to leave you or to turn back from you. Where you go I will go, and where you stay I will stay. Your people will be my people and your God my God. Where you die I will die, and there I will be buried. May the Lord deal with me, be it ever so severely, if anything but death separates you and me."

MI
TPD Read **Ruth 1:6-18**
SM

1 Both of Naomi's daughters-in-law loved her, but they made very different decisions about how to go on with their lives. How did Orpah and Ruth's responses differ?

2 Why do you think Ruth wanted to go with Naomi?

3 Look at Ruth's words in **Ruth 1:16-17**. Do you have this kind of unconditional love for those in your family?

TPD
SM **Hard to love?**
WO
Can it be hard to love families sometimes?

What things could make it difficult for someone to feel love for their family?

What things could make it difficult for someone to show love to their family?

Share your ideas with a partner.

Com
BC Write a poem or prayer that a Christian might read in a church service. Include:
SM

• The desire to love others as Ruth loved Naomi.

• Confession for not loving those who are difficult to love.

Authority

What is authority?

Authority is the right to exercise power and control over a person, a group of people or a situation. Authority also includes the responsibility to make decisions. The word can be used in different ways:

- 'The headmaster **has authority** over the entire school.'
- 'The headmaster **is** the main **authority** in the school.'
- 'There are several **figures of authority** in this school: the teachers, the vice-principals and the headmaster.'
- 'If you carry on breaking the law I will have to notify **the authorities**.'

There are many people who have authority over us in different situations. This means that they should make decisions about what is best for us. They create rules and standards which we are expected to obey.

MI
TPD
SM
PD

Would you like to be in authority in your classroom? Copy the table below and list the things you would have control over and the things you would have responsibility for.

Things I have control over	Things I am responsible for
How much homework we are given	Make sure everyone in the class is safe

You may wish to ask your teacher for ideas.

MI
WO
Cit

In **pairs**, make a list of all the people who have authority over you.

Com
TPD
Cit
PD

Why are the following people given authority?

- Police Officers
- Teachers
- Parents
- Judges

List the reasons why each are given authority, then discuss your ideas as a class.

Why obey authority?

Sometimes we can find it hard to obey or respect authority, particularly if we do not agree with its decisions. So why should we obey authority?

Com
TPD
Cit

Read the following scenario and discuss the questions as a class.

If a house catches fire, someone will dial 999 and the emergency services will arrive shortly after. They will do several things to keep the situation under control.

- Police will cordon off the area and prevent anybody from going too near the fire.

- Paramedics will attend to the injured.
- The fire brigade will put out the fire while rescuing anybody who is trapped inside the burning building.

1 Why do you think the victims of disasters choose to follow the instructions and advice of the emergency services?

2 In what other situations is it necessary to follow instructions and do exactly as you are told?

3 What would happen if people did not do as they are told in these situations?

Christians believe that God is the creator of the universe and has authority over all things within it. God has the right to judge all men and women and God should be obeyed. God does not force human beings to obey, but gives each individual a choice.

In the story of Adam and Eve we read of the first human beings created by God. At first everything is perfect, but the man and woman are tempted to disobey the rules God gave them.

MI
TPD
SM

Read **Genesis 3** and answer the following questions:

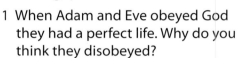

1 When Adam and Eve obeyed God they had a perfect life. Why do you think they disobeyed?

2 Why do Adam and Eve hide from God?

3 How does God react?

The serpent who tempts Eve in Genesis 3 is usually thought to represent the Devil.

Com
TPD
PD

Can you think of a time when you were tempted to do something wrong?

Get into **pairs** and discuss what happened and how you might best deal with the situation should it happen again.

In the Bible we see two ways in which people live their lives:

- **The way of obedience** – 'God's way is the best way. I want to please God. I will do whatever he tells me to do.'

- **The way of rebellion** – 'I want to please myself. I will do what I want to do. I don't care who else gets hurt'

The New Testament teaches that authorities like governments have been put in place by God. People have nothing to fear from these authorities if they do good.

> 'Obey your leaders and submit to their authority. They keep watch over you as men who must give an account. Obey them so that their work will be a joy, not a burden, for that would be of no advantage to you.'
>
> (**Hebrews 13:17**)

> 'Everyone must submit himself to the governing authorities, for there is no authority except that which God has established. The authorities that exist have been established by God. Consequently, he who rebels against the authority is rebelling against what God has instituted, and those who do so will bring judgment on themselves. For rulers hold no terror for those who do right, but for those who do wrong. Do you want to be free from fear of the one in authority? Then do what is right and he will commend you.'
>
> (**Romans 13:1-3**)

Com / TPD / PD

The Bible teaches that it is good to show respect to those in authority, as this will give glory to God.

Think of ways in which you could show respect to the following authorities:

- Your teachers
- Your headmaster
- Your parents
- The police

TPD / SM / PD

The American writer and politician Benjamin Franklin drew up some practical suggestions for showing respect to others:

- The best thing to give your enemy is forgiveness;
- to an opponent, tolerance;
- to a friend, your ear;
- to your child, a good example;
- to a father, reverence;
- to your mother, conduct that will make her proud of you;
- to yourself, respect;
- to everyone, charity.

Do you agree with Benjamin Franklin? Would you find any of these suggestions very difficult?

Try rewriting these suggestions in your own words.

Respect

It is important that we are able to respect those with authority over us. We will not always agree with every decision or rule made by those in authority, but we should still acknowledge the difficult job they often have.

Com / TPD / WO / Cit / PD

'We live in a world in which respect for authority is decreasing.'

Organise a class debate on this statement.

You will need to hear the views of people who agree and people who disagree.

Back up your views using evidence from real life.

Finish the debate with a class vote.

Com
MI
SM
WO
Cit

Research Project.

Talk to an older person and ask them questions about their school days. Create a folder or booklet on this person and their experiences.

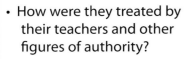

- How were they treated by their teachers and other figures of authority?
- How did they feel about authority? Did they respect it?
- How have times changed since then?

MI
BC
SM
WO
Cit
PD

You only need to watch the news on television or read a newspaper to discover the way in which authority is viewed by our society.

Get into groups of **four** and follow these instructions:

- Look through some newspapers and magazines and cut out any headlines or stories which you think illustrate a lack of respect for authority.
- Make a poster by sticking these cut-outs to a large piece of card.

'Hi, my name is Liz and I'm an Art teacher. Often pupils tell me that they do respect their teachers and parents, but that sometimes they don't get the chance to speak and are accused of arguing or being cheeky.'

Learning to respect authority and the decisions of others is an important lesson everyone must learn. There are seven simple actions you can practise to help you to act respectfully toward others:

1. Look at the person who is talking to you. Looking at a person shows that you are paying attention.

   Helpful hints:
   - Don't stare or make faces.
   - Don't look away.
   - Listening carefully will help you understand what the other person is saying.

2. Remain calm and monitor your feelings and behaviour. By staying calm, you can hear exactly what the other person is saying.

3. If a person says something you don't agree with, don't react negatively by whining, crying or arguing. That can make the situation worse. If you do feel you are losing your temper, take deep breaths or excuse yourself from the situation until you calm down.

4. Use a pleasant or neutral tone of voice. Others are more likely to listen to you if you use a pleasant tone. Speak slowly and clearly, and use short sentences. Try to smile. People are more comfortable talking with someone who is friendly. Acknowledge the person's decision by saying 'Okay' or 'Yes, I understand.'

5. Make sure you wait until the person has finished talking before you say or do anything. It is usually best to answer, but sometimes nodding your head will be enough to show the person you understand.

6. Possibly disagree at a later time. If you disagree right away, you will appear to be arguing. Instead, take some time to plan how you will approach the person who made the decision or gave the instruction that you didn't agree with. Plan in advance what you are going to say. After you have spoken, thank the person for listening, regardless of the final outcome.

7. Avoid arguing, sulking or becoming angry.

Not all decisions made by those in authority will be in your favour, and you will sometimes have to do things you don't enjoy. However, by learning how to accept decisions with maturity, you will learn from those experiences and improve the chances for better outcomes in the future.

Com
WO
PD

As a class, discuss the following questions.

1 Is it always easy to agree with what parents and teachers want and expect from you?

2 Is it possible to have a different opinion from someone but still respect them?

Questioning authority

Is it always right to obey those in authority?

What if someone in authority orders you to do something you know is wrong?

Com
TPD
Cit
PD

Read the following story and discuss with a partner.

Stephen had just started work in a computer supply company. A client ordered a hard drive but when it arrived the manager discovered he had made a mistake. He had ordered the wrong one. He told Stephen to send it back.

'Tell them it's damaged.'

'But, it isn't damaged.' Stephen replied.

The manager dropped the hard drive on the floor, then handed it back to Stephen.

'It's damaged now. Send it back.'

What would you do if you were in Stephen's situation? What *should* he do?

The Bible teaches that Christians should 'submit to authority' **(Hebrews 13:2)**, but there are many times in the Bible when God's people choose not to obey laws that go against God. In **Acts 4:18-20** two disciples are threatened and ordered not to tell others about Jesus:

> 'Then they called them in again and commanded them not to speak or teach at all in the name of Jesus. But Peter and John replied, 'Judge for yourselves whether it is right in God's sight to obey you rather than God. For we cannot help speaking about what we have seen and heard."

There are some countries today where the government has declared Christianity illegal. Christians break the law by meeting in secret. If they are caught worshipping they are thrown in prison without a trial and in some cases executed. This is called **persecution**.

In situations like this it is difficult for Christians to obey those in authority.

TPD
SM
Cit
PD

Is there anything that you believe in so much that you would risk being executed for it?

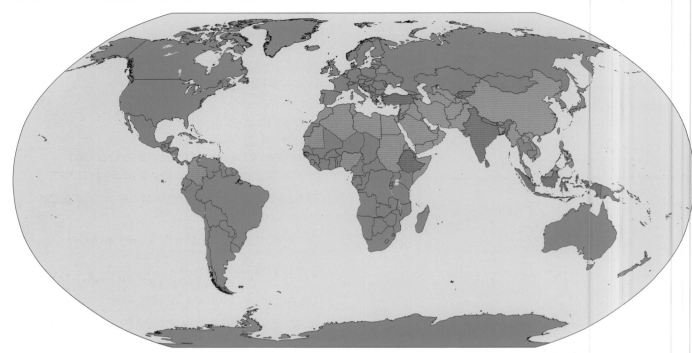

This map highlights countries where Christians are persecuted. Countries where Christianity is restricted by the government are shown in orange. Countries where Christians suffer violence because of their beliefs are shown in red.

ICT
MI
SM

Find out about countries where the authorities have made Christianity illegal. You can start by visiting **www.persecution.org**.

Present your findings to the class in the form of a report, or make a poster showing how Christians are restricted in different countries.

In the book of Daniel, we read about how Daniel's friends Shadrach, Meshach and Abednego disobeyed the king. They would not bow down to a golden idol even though they knew they would be severely punished.

King Nebuchadnezzar threatened to throw the three men into a furnace, but they still refused to worship something other than God:

> 'Shadrach, Meshach and Abednego replied to the king, 'O Nebuchadnezzar, we do not need to defend ourselves before you in this matter. If we are thrown into the blazing furnace, the God we serve is able to save us from it, and he will rescue us from your hand, O king, But even if he does not, we want you to know, O king, that we will not serve your gods or worship the image of gold you have set up'

(Daniel 3:16-18)

MI
BC
WO

Read **Daniel 3.**

In groups of six, write and perform a role-play based on the story of the Fiery Furnace.

Here are some tips to help you:

• Maybe you should split your role-play into several different scenes. Quite a lot happens in this story, so think about how exactly you will present it without confusing your audience.

- Will you use props in your performance? For example, how will you represent the idol and the fire?
- Will you use modern day language or will you use the exact words from the Bible?

Here are some examples of Christian rule-breakers who have risked being sent to jail, tortured or put to death for their faith.

Photo courtesy of Billy Graham Evangelistic Association

1 During the Second World War, **Corrie ten Boom** and her family hid Jews from the Nazi government in a secret room in their house. They were captured and imprisoned in concentration camps, where most of them died. After her release in 1944, Corrie ten Boom continued to help the persecuted by setting up rehabilitation centres and speaking at conferences all over the world.

2 For over fifty years, **Open Doors** have smuggled bibles into all parts of the world such as China and the Soviet Union. The organisation was started by a missionary named **Brother Andrew**. His courageous exploits earned him the nickname 'God's Smuggler'.

Picture Source Open Doors UK © 2009

Com ICT BC SM

Find out as much information as you can about one of the following: Corrie Ten Boom; Brother Andrew; Open Doors; or another similar organisation. You can research on the internet or in a library.

Present your findings in a written report, complete with pictures. You should include:

- Some background information on the person or group.
- Details of the government they worked against.
- What kind of risks were they taking by smuggling bibles, hiding refugees, etc.?
- What would have happened to them if they were caught?
- Where is this person or organisation now?
- What have they changed by their work? How will they be remembered?

TPD WO Cit PD

Discuss with a partner:

Why did these people think it was all right to break the rules?

Can you think of any situations where disobeying authority would be the right thing to do?

Jesus: Rule-breaker?

Jesus was often in conflict with the religious and political authorities he encountered during his ministry. The **Pharisees** were a strict religious group who often criticised Jesus for his actions and his message. They did not like it when people claimed he was the Son of God, and they were suspicious of the miracles he performed. In the end they had Jesus executed.

The Pharisees misused their religious authority, taking the

Ten Commandments and adding hundreds of other rules for people to follow.

In **John 5:1-15** we read that Jesus healed a disabled man at the Bethesda pool in Jerusalem. This annoyed the Pharisees greatly. Jesus performed the miracle on the Sabbath - a day on which no work was to be done.

Com
MI
BC
SM

Read **John 5:1-15** and answer the following questions:

1. Imagine you are the crippled man at the Bethesda pool in Jerusalem. Write a detailed account about your encounter with Jesus. You should mention:
   - What your life was like before meeting Jesus.
   - How you felt when he spoke to you.
   - What it was like to be healed after being paralysed for so many years.
   - How you felt when the Pharisees attacked Jesus for helping you.
   - How your life has been transformed since the event.

2. Imagine you are one of the Pharisees. Write a detailed letter to another Pharisee explaining why you believe Jesus must be stopped. You should mention:
   - The fact that Jesus is performing miracles on the Sabbath.
   - You are unhappy that people are claiming he is the Son of God.
   - You are worried what effect Jesus' miracles and words will have on the Jewish people. What if he tries to bring down the government?

TPD
SM

On another similar occasion, when the Pharisees accused Jesus of breaking the Sabbath law, he tells them:

   'The Sabbath was made for man, not man for the Sabbath' (**Mark 2:27**)

What do you think Jesus means by this?

What does it say about rules and authority?

Parents

As a teenager, the people with the ultimate authority over you and the ultimate responsibility for you are most likely to be your parents or guardians.

Relationships with parents are a potential source of both frustration and fulfilment for teenagers. It is important to love and respect your parents, but does this mean that you must obey them at all times?

Kate's Diary

Kate is eighteen. She is just about to start her 'A' levels, but she is more keen on going out with her friends and having fun than revising for her exams. This causes problems with her parents, which Kate writes about in her diary.

13th April

– Stayed over at Jenny's house at the weekend. Mum and Dad would kill me if they knew that her parents are still on holiday. I lied and told them that they had come home early. I feel a bit guilty as they do trust me, but they don't really like Jenny and I wanted to stay over.

Went to a club in town with some of the girls from school. I met the nicest guy – his name is Rick, he's 20 and an apprentice mechanic. Couldn't believe it when he came over and asked me to dance; Jenny was so jealous! He took my number but he probably won't call.

17th April

– Can't get to sleep – too excited! Rick called and asked me out at the weekend. Only one problem – the parents!

20th April

– Major row with Mum today – she says I shouldn't go out so near to my exams, but I can't work all the time. I can't believe that they're actually trying to control who I see. I'm totally fed up. Mum and I used to get on so well, but we seem to argue all the time now. I hate her.

22nd April

– Went out with Rick again last night. All his friends were there with their girlfriends and they looked so mature and glamorous. I didn't want them to think I was a freak so I just kept on taking the drinks that were put in front of me.

I threw up in the car on the way home and Rick was a bit annoyed with me. We didn't get home until after 3 am. All the lights were on – Mum and Dad had waited up for me. They went mad when they saw the state I was in, and Dad and Rick had words. Why can't they understand the pressure they are putting me under?

9th May

– Had my first exam today – what a disaster. Jenny thought the paper was okay but I hadn't a clue. I just can't cope any more. Mum and Dad want me to do Medicine at university, but I really want to do Art. I'm going to fail everything so I probably won't even go to university. At least Rick loves me – I couldn't cope without him.

18th May

– Life has become unbearable at home. Mum and Dad have been like prison wardens. We had another major bust up tonight. They said I couldn't go out with Rick because I have an exam at the end of the week. I totally lost it and threw a few things into a bag and left. Mum was so upset but I'm past caring – I can't live at home any more. Rick took me to his flat and I'm going to stay there.

25th May

– I've seen a really different side to Rick since we started living together. He's so moody and I didn't realise how much he drinks. We had a big row last night and he put his fist through the living room door. I was really scared but what can I do? I can't go home! I think I've made a terrible mistake.

MI TPD SM PD

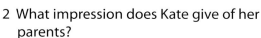

Answer the following questions in your classwork book.

1. What are the main causes of conflict in this family?
2. What impression does Kate give of her parents?
3. Do you think Kate should have obeyed her parents? Explain your answer.
4. Why do you think teenagers often challenge their parents' authority?

BC SM PD

Pretend you are Kate's mother. Write a diary entry for each of the days that Kate wrote one. What are the main differences in their point of view?

TPD SM WO PD

Should children obey their parents without question in all circumstances? What if a father told his son to go into a shop and steal something?

Can you think of other occasions when obeying parents might be difficult or wrong?

Discuss your ideas with a partner.

One writer summed up how teenagers should behave towards their parents:

> 'Love always, obey usually, communicate regularly, question occasionally, defy only when it is clearly wrong to obey.'

Prejudice, Discrimination and Reconciliation

Prejudice

'We are each burdened with prejudice: against the poor or the rich, the smart or the slow, the gaunt or the obese. It is natural to develop prejudices. It is noble to rise above them.'

Anonymous

Prejudice comes from the Latin word *praejudicium*, meaning **previous judgement**.

When we **prejudge**, we make assumptions based on very little knowledge. For example, someone might dislike a person because of the clothes they are wearing or the colour of their skin, without knowing anything about their personality. They might be generous, loving and friendly, but are not given a proper chance to show the kind of person they are.

Prejudice normally refers to a negative attitude formed about a person or group of people.

Com
TPD
WO
Cit
PD

Get into groups and discuss the following questions. If you are really honest, you will have a better discussion.

1 What different types of prejudice can you think of?

2 Have you ever experienced any form of prejudice?

3 Have you ever shown prejudice to someone else?

How Do We Become Prejudiced?

People are not born prejudiced, so where do we get these negative attitudes from?

Children learn almost everything they know from their parents, including beliefs. Often they do not question their parents' opinions, even if they are offensive or harmful to others. It may be difficult to admit to having absorbed our parent's views.

TPD
SM
Cit
PD

Can you think of any prejudices or attitudes which you may have copied from your parents or family?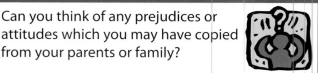

A **stereotype** is a fixed idea that people have about what someone or something is like. It is often negative, and might be based on a previous bad experience. For example, we might have met someone from a town in Northern Ireland who was rude to us, and we therefore form a **stereotype** that all people from that town are rude.

A stereotype can also be an opinion that you form about someone when you see them for the first time. For example, we might not like the way they style their hair or the clothes they choose. A stereotype can affect how you treat that person.

As teenagers, we spend more and more time with our friends. Without realising it, we might begin to take on their prejudices too. We might copy the things our friends say and do, even if this behaviour is hurtful towards other people.

Why do we accept prejudice?

Here are some possible reasons:

- It might be that we are afraid of standing up to people in case they start being nasty to us.
- It might be that we do not want to look uncool and be left out of the group.
- Younger children may feel that their parents will be pleased if they believe the same things as they do.
- It might simply be because we do not know any better. We have not taken the time to stop and think whether what we believe is right or wrong.

Stereotypes

'If you judge people you have no time to love them.'
Mother Teresa

MI
TPD
WO
PD

Look at the two photographs and answer the questions.

1 Which of the men has the most respectable appearance?

2 Get into pairs. One person should write a short descriptive paragraph of the man on the left while the other should write one describing the man on the right. You should mention:
- What age the men are.
- Where they come from.
- What they do for a living.

3 Compare your descriptions. Are they different or similar?

Would it surprise you know that both of these photographs are of the same person? The photograph on the right is of this man going to work as an engineer. The other was taken when he was a student.

Com
TPD
EfE
PD

Imagine that two very different people have gone to the bank to take out a loan. Based on appearances only, discuss how the bank manager would react to the following:

1 A scruffy student girl with ripped jeans and a tongue stud .

2 A man in a smart business suit, shiny black shoes and a wedding ring.

Making Assumptions

A famous saying states, 'You should never judge a book by its cover.'

This means you cannot really judge people or situations until you know them well. It is pointless and silly to look at somebody we do not know and believe that we can immediately tell everything about their interests, sense of humour, background, family life, concerns or any other aspects of their personality.

Com
TPD
WO
Cit
PD

In pairs, discuss the questions:

1 What do you think when you look at this lady? List words that you could use to describe her.

2 What kind of person do you think she is?

3 Do you know anything about her family? Do you know what food she likes? Do you know if she has a sense of humour?

4 Why is it dangerous to make assumptions?

TPD
SM

1 Did you ever have an idea about somebody which turned out to be completely wrong?

2 Did someone ever think something completely wrong about you?

The way in which we form assumptions affects our relationships with people who are different to us in some way. We might have:

• **Different backgrounds**. They might be poor and we might be rich, or vice versa.

• **Different religions**. They might go to a different church than us, or have a different faith.

• **Different race**. They might have come here from another country, or they might have been born here to parents from another country.

Read the following short story. It might explain the idea of making assumptions more clearly.

Once, a tiny mouse crawled along the floor of a dense jungle. She hopped over grass and struggled over rocks, twitching her whiskers as she went.

Suddenly, the mouse spied a great lion, sleeping in the afternoon sun. She admired the lion's strong muscles, his long whiskers and his impressive mane.

'He's fast asleep,' thought the mouse to herself as she clambered up onto the lion's tail, scurried across his back and towards the soft bush of hair.

With that, the lion awoke, and quickly caught the mouse in his paw.

'Please,' squeaked the mouse, feeling the sharp claws closing around her body. 'Let me go and someday I'll come back and help you.'

The lion laughed out loud. 'You are so small!' he bellowed, roaring with delight. 'How could you ever help me?'

The lion rolled onto his back, laughing and rubbing his belly. The mouse jumped to freedom and ran until she was far, far away.

The next day, two hunters arrived in the jungle. They went to the lion's lair and set up a huge snare made out of rope and branches. When the lion came home later that night, he stepped into the snare. The snare snapped shut, catching him in the trap.

The lion roared and twisted and cried, but he couldn't pull himself free.

The mouse heard the commotion and immediately came running to the scene. She saw the lion wrapped up in ropes as thick as jungle vines. She spied the one rope that held the trap together. She nibbled and nibbled until it broke. The lion

was able to shake off all of the other ropes that held him tight. He stood up, shook his mane and let out one loud roar.

Then the great lion looked down at the little mouse. 'Dear friend,' he said, 'I was foolish to ridicule you for being small. You helped save my life, and for that I will be forever thankful.'

MI TPD SM

1 What did the lion learn in this story?

2 Do you think the mouse was right to help the lion? Explain your answer.

Discrimination

'I would like to be known as a person who is concerned about freedom and equality and justice and prosperity for all people.'
Rosa Parks

Discrimination means treating people differently because of their gender, race, religion or background. Discrimination happens when people allow their prejudices and assumptions to affect their behaviour towards others.

If we were honest, we would admit that we all have prejudiced thoughts now and again. Unfortunately, some people actually put these feelings into action. This can mean treating others cruelly, using bad language or behaving violently towards those who are different.

In your History lessons, you might have heard about how African Americans were treated in the United States because of the colour of their skin. During the 1940s and 1950s certain parts of America were greatly affected by discrimination. African American people were not allowed into certain cafés, restaurants and cinemas. They were not even allowed to ride on some buses because these were reserved for white people.

Many people protested against the injustice that they saw in America. One of the most famous was **Rosa Parks**.

Rosa Parks was a forty-two year old African American lady from Alabama. On 1 December 1955 Rosa was taking a bus home from work. She was sitting in the area reserved for white people. The bus was very busy, and when the driver ordered Rosa to move so that a white passenger could take her seat, she refused to do so.

Rosa was dragged off the bus, arrested for disturbing the police and later sent to court, but

this small action had an important effect on the system of discrimination in America. By standing up against a system that she believed to be cruel and wrong, Rosa helped to change the way people thought about discriminating against others.

Sectarianism

'Prejudices are the chains forged by ignorance to keep men apart.'

Marguerite Gardiner

Sectarianism is prejudice against someone with the same religion who practises some parts of that religion differently.

We have all heard of sectarianism between Protestants and Catholics. They are both part of the Christian religion, but they believe different things. Just as there are Protestants and Catholics in Christianity, there are also Sunni Muslims and Shia Muslims, Orthodox Jews and Reform Jews.

Religious differences often cause rivalry and hostility between two groups. It can take the form of name-calling, telling jokes, offensive songs and chants, or other forms of verbal abuse. Some people don't think that sectarian jokes or rivalry should be taken that seriously, but in some cases, sectarianism has led to violent attacks and murder.

There is a long history of conflict in Northern Ireland between Catholics and Protestants. You may have heard of the term 'The Troubles', which is used to describe the years of fighting between 1969 and 1998.

During these years over three and a half thousand people were killed from both Protestant and Catholic communities.

Enniskillen, 1987

In 1987 a bomb planted by the IRA exploded during a Remembrance Day service in Enniskillen, County Fermanagh. Eleven people were killed, and at least sixty-three others were injured, nine of them seriously. Thirteen children were harmed in the blast. The dead included three married couples, a retired policemen and a nurse.

There was an immediate public outcry against the bombing. Archbishop Robin Eames, head of the Church of Ireland, said, 'I wished the bombers could have seen what I have seen.' Many demanded that the IRA give up those who were responsible, so they could be brought to justice. Others called for more extreme forms of punishment.

However, amidst the tragedy one man acted for good and changed the course of events entirely. Gordon Wilson, whose daughter Marie was killed in the attack, told the BBC, 'I have lost my daughter, and we shall miss her. But I bear no ill will. I bear no grudge. Dirty sort of talk is not going to bring her back to life.' Wilson said he forgave her killers, adding, 'I shall pray for those people tonight and every night.'

Right: The Enniskillen War Memorial. A dove was added for each person who died in the 1987 bomb.

Read the story and answer these questions.

1 How hard do you think it was for Gordon Wilson to forgive the bombers? Give reasons for your answer.

2 Why do you think Gordon Wilson forgave those who had killed his daughter?

3 Do you think you could forgive someone who killed a member of your family?

4 Do you think that Gordon Wilson was helped by his Christian faith? Explain your answer.

5 Is Gordon Wilson a good example for others? Explain why you think this.

What does 'The Troubles' mean to you?

How do you feel when you hear that there was violence in this country for thirty years?

Why do you think it happened?

How can we make sure it never happens again?

In Jesus' day there was sectarianism between the Jews and the Samaritans. They had once been one race and one religion but now they were separate. The two groups hated each other so much that Jews would travel for miles rather than journey through Samaria.

Jesus tells a famous story about a good Samaritan who helps and injured man. People would have been shocked to hear about a Samaritan helping a Jewish person.

The Parable of the Good Samaritan
(Luke 10:30-37)

''A man was going down from Jerusalem to Jericho, when he fell into the hands of robbers. They stripped him of his clothes, beat him and went away, leaving him half dead. A priest happened to be going down the same road, and when he saw the man, he passed by on the other side. So too, a Levite, when he came to the place and saw him, passed by on the other side. But a Samaritan, as he travelled, came where the man was; and when he saw him, he took pity on him. He went to him and bandaged his wounds, pouring on oil and wine. Then he put the man on his own donkey, took him to an inn and took care of him. The next day he took out two silver coins and gave them to the innkeeper. 'Look after him,' he said, 'and when I return, I will reimburse you for any extra expense you may have.''

Jesus concluded, 'Which of these three do you think was a neighbour to the man who fell into the hands of robbers?'

The expert in the law replied, 'The one who had mercy on him.'

Jesus told him, 'Go and do likewise.''

MI TPD SM PD

Carefully read the passage again then answer the following questions:

1 Why do you think the priest and the Levite ignored the injured man?

2 Why do you think the Samaritan helped him?

3 List the ways in which the Samaritan was kind to the man.

4 Why do you think Jesus told this story? What was he trying to say?

5 How would you act if you saw a helpless man on the way home from school? Would you stop to help him?

MI BC

Create a comic strip retelling the story of the Good Samaritan.

– How many frames will you need?

– How will you draw each of the main characters?

– Will you use speech bubbles, or include text from the Bible?

MI BC WO

Get into groups of **three**.

Think of a group of people who might face discrimination, or are sometimes viewed negatively, just as the Samaritans were.

Write and perform a short drama featuring this group, based on the story of the Good Samaritan.

You can change some of the details as long as your drama gives the same message as Jesus' parable.

Racism

'If we were to wake up some morning and find that everyone was the same race, creed and colour, we would find some other causes for prejudice by noon.'
George Aiken

An **ethnic minority** is a group of people of a certain race, religion or nationality who live in a country where most people belong to a **different** race, religion or nationality.

For example, white people in China would be considered an ethnic minority. Equally, a person of Chinese race would be considered an ethnic minority in Northern Ireland.

A number of ethnic minority communities have been living in Northern Ireland for a long time

For example, some people of Chinese race have lived in Northern Ireland all their lives. Their parents have lived here all *their* lives.

ICT
MI
SM

There are many thousands of people living in Northern Ireland as members of ethnic minorities. They include people from **India**, **China**, **Poland**, **Portugal** and other countries.

1 Write down as much as you know about each of these communities.
 • Where in the world is their native country?
 • How many people live there?
 • How many of these people live in Northern Ireland?
 • What is their main religion?
 • What sorts of jobs do they do?

2 Use the internet or library to research these same communities and then answer the questions again.

3 Consider how your answers have changed.
 • Did you find out anything new about these communities?
 • Did you discover anything surprising?
 • Were you surprised how little / how much you knew about other ethnic communities?

Racism is the belief that one ethnic group is inferior to another. Racism exists all over the world, sadly including our own country.

Fransuer comes from Africa and teaches Religious Education in a school in Belfast. He describes how he has found living in Northern Ireland:

'Generally, this is a great place to live. However, about five percent of people I've come across are racist.

There are two main types of discrimination that I have faced in this part of the world. The first one is simply having young fellows shout unpleasant insults from cars. I'm used to that. But one of the most upsetting examples of racism was in a supermarket in Belfast where another university student did monkey gestures at me.

Other types of racism are more subtle – like through jokes that are race-based. I feel more sorry for the perpetrators of racism. My sadness is for those who stoop so low.'

Fransuer describes the unpleasant experience of being the butt of a racist joke. Some people might think that this kind of behaviour is harmless, but racism can lead on to more serious problems, such as verbal and physical abuse. Many ethnic minorities face discrimination, threats and violence.

Read the following newspaper article about the spread of racism in Northern Ireland.

Race Hate On The Rise

Racist attacks regularly take place in Northern Ireland. In fact, some have even named it the race hate capital of Europe. It has been argued that in recent years racism has become a bigger problem than sectarianism.

Police reports indicate that racially motivated incidents include offensive graffiti and physical attacks. The most disturbing aspect is that several of these attacks have been on the most vulnerable members of these communities: children, pregnant women, Filipino nurses and Muslim women.

Numbers of patrols have increased in areas where Chinese and Pakistani families live, but people are still choosing to leave their homes after receiving verbal and physical threats.

Patrick Yu, a representative for the Northern Ireland Council for Ethnic Minorities, put forward the bad news that the reality is actually much worse. 'A lot of cases are not reported to the police for one reason or another. In particular they are more vulnerable to reprisal if they report them to the police,' Yu said. 'We need to educate people about the multiculturalism now in Northern Ireland. We have more than two communities.'

Contrary to what statistics might suggest, not all areas of our society are negative towards our ethnic neighbours. Most notable is the Dungannon newspaper that has begun a regular column in both Portuguese and English. Ian Greer, editor for the Tyrone Courier, commented, 'The Portuguese are now a sizeable group that has come along in the past four to five years, and is an important part of life in Dungannon.'

If only more began to follow Greer's example, then we could avoid Northern Ireland's growing reputation as a violent and unwelcoming country.

Story taken from http://news.bbc.co.uk/2/hi/uk_news/northern_ireland/3390249.stm, accessed 22 July, 2009.

Com TPD WO Cit PD

Get into groups and discuss the following questions:

1 How can some people in Northern Ireland be described as racist?

2 How does it make you feel when you read about the ways in which members of ethnic minorities are treated in our country?

3 Do you think that it is ever right to discriminate against someone because of the ethnic group they belong to?

EFFECTS OF PREJUDICE AND DISCRIMINATION

Anger and Violence

As we have seen, prejudice and discrimination can have a destructive effect on society. If we are discriminated against for any reason, then it is understandable that we might feel angry.

Some people take this even further and long for revenge. They commit terrible acts of violence, claiming that what they are doing is right and excusable because they were wronged first.

Com TPD SM WO Cit

1 Can you think of any examples when people have responded violently to discrimination? Maybe an event you have read about in History or something that you have heard about on the news?

2 Do you think that violence is ever the right answer to prejudice? Discuss this question in pairs, then share your thoughts with the rest of the class.

3 If you were a prejudiced person, what effect might your behaviour have on your family and friends?

Com
TPD
WO
Cit
PD

In pairs list as many examples of exclusion as you can think of.

For example, are there any sports that girls are excluded from?

Exclusion

Those who are **included** are those who are a part of a group. Those who are **excluded** are not allowed to be part of that group. You have already read about how African Americans were excluded from certain areas of American society. The same sort of thing happens in many places in the world.

TPD
SM
PD

Exclusion does not always happen on purpose. People do not always mean to leave out those who are different.

How can you make sure that you are inclusive and friendly to people who are different from you?

Com
WO
PD

Forming groups

Clear a space in the middle of the class. The teacher will be in charge of this activity. The rest of the class should walk around the room and wait for instructions.

The teacher will call out an instruction to help the class to get into groups. For example:

- 'Get into groups of eye colour'. Those with blue eyes should form one group, green eyes a second group, and brown eyes a third.
- 'Get into groups of four people.'
- 'Get into groups of those who wear glasses and those who don't'.
- 'Get into groups of six people.'
- 'Get into groups of hair colour: blond, brown, red and black'.
- 'Get into groups of three people.'

1 Discuss how you felt to be in the different groups. How did you feel if:
  - You were in a smaller group?
  - You were in a larger group?
  - When you were in the groups that formed numbers; did you get into groups of friends? Did anyone not manage to get into a group at all? How would it have felt to be standing by yourself when everybody else was in a group?

2 Think about your lives and the experiences of others. Can you describe a time when you really felt that you were included in a group? Or a time when you felt excluded?

3 Have you ever excluded other people, even if you didn't mean to?

Reconciliation

When people try to forget their differences, sort out their arguments and become friends again this is called **reconciliation**. Throughout the world there are many charities devoted to reconciling broken communities and working in countries affected by warfare. For example, several organisations in Northern Ireland work in areas that have been split apart by violence and cruelty.

One of the most important developments for reconciliation in Northern Ireland has been the start of **integrated education**. Most schools teach either mainly Protestant pupils or mainly Catholic pupils. Integrated schools welcome both Protestants and Catholics as well as those from other faiths. In a school like this, children are encouraged to accept each other's differences and learn about each other's culture.

Lagan College, Belfast was the first planned integrated school in Northern Ireland.

What do you think the doves on their badge represent?

MI TPD SM

Find out as much as you can about an integrated school. If you go to an integrated school you can write about your own.

1 Do you go to an integrated school?
   • If **yes**, do you like going there? What do you like about it?
   • If **no**, would you like to go to one?
2 Choose an integrated school and find out about it.
   • When was it set up?
   • Why was it set up?
   • Does it have a motto?
3 Do you think that integrated schools are a good idea? Explain your answer.

CHRISTIANS AND RECONCILIATION

The Bible repeatedly teaches that Christians are to love and accept others regardless of their background. God's love is for everyone, not just a select few.

In the book of **Acts** we read about a division that appeared at the very beginning of the Church. The first followers of Jesus were all Jews. Many did not believe that they should include those who were not Jewish.

When **Gentiles** (non-Jews) started to become Christians, some Jewish Christians refused to eat with them. The new Gentile Christians did not keep the Jewish food laws. This caused division.

TPD Can you imagine what it would have been like to be a Gentile Christian at this time? Why might you have felt excluded?

In **Acts 10** we read how Peter, a Jewish Christian and one of the original disciples, was challenged by God about holding such prejudiced attitudes. Whilst up on the roof, Peter saw a vision of a sheet that was full of all kinds of animals. Some of these animals were those that Jews were forbidden to eat.

However, God spoke to Peter in the vision, saying 'Get up, Peter. Kill and eat' and 'Do not call anything impure that God has made clean'.

Shortly after, Peter was called to visit a man named Cornelius, a centurion and a Gentile who was well known for his strong Christian faith.

While speaking with Cornelius, Peter realised the meaning of his vision: just as people should not call the animals God made unclean, so they should not call human beings unclean. Sectarian differences were not important to God, so there should be no division between Jewish and Gentile believers.

'Then Peter began to speak: 'I now realise how true it is that God does not show favouritism but accepts men from every nation who fear him and do what is right'

(**Acts 10:34-35**)

Peter's vision from God challenged his sectarian views.

MI
TPD
SM

Read **Acts 10**.

Copy out and complete the following boxes.

Peter's Profile

From: _____

Religion: _____

Occupation: _____

How did God speak to him? _____
_____

What did he do next? _____

What effect did this have? _____
_____

Cornelius' Profile

From: _____

Religion: _____

Occupation: _____

How did God speak to him? _____
_____

What did he do next? _____

What effect did this have? _____
_____

People with Special Needs

The term **people with special needs** usually refers to those with learning difficulties or a disability of some kind. A **disability** is a physical or mental condition that has a serious or long-term effect on a person's ability to carry out daily tasks.

This diagram shows the four main types of disability:

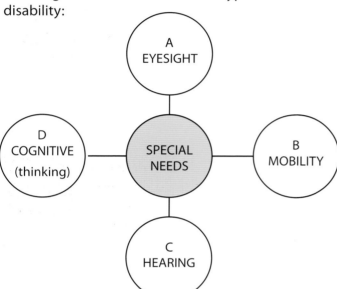

MI
TPD
SM

Copy out the diagram above and insert the correct definitions from the list below.

1 This includes people with no vision, or some vision; people with colour blindness and those with eyesight problems related to ageing.

2 This includes people who are completely deaf or have partial hearing in one or both ears and need to use a hearing aid.

3 This describes a wide range of different types of physical disabilities, eg Multiple Sclerosis (MS), Parkinson's Disease or a stroke.

4 This refers to everything from severe learning difficulties to mild dyslexia – a condition where people have problems with reading, writing or spelling.

The Bible and people with Special Needs

In our society disability can affect all people regardless of their social background but in the New Testament people with disabilities were usually poor. Their condition made it impossible for them to get a job.

The Jews at that time regarded any kind of sickness as a punishment for sin, so disabled people were often rejected by the rest of society. It was believed that they must have committed some terrible sin for which they were being punished. They would be forced to beg at the side of the street and in public meeting places.

Jesus challenged people's opinions by teaching that disabilities were not a punishment for sin (**John 9:3**). He spent much of his time with people that the rest of society had rejected, including the disabled.

Mark 2:1-12 tells the story of some men who wanted to bring their disabled friend to Jesus. Jesus was inside a house and it was crowded out onto the street. The men were so determined that they dug a hole through the roof of the house and lowered their friend in on a mat.

MI TPD SM

Read **Mark 2:1-12**

1 Why could the men not get their friend to Jesus?

2 Why might Jesus have told the man 'Your sins are forgiven'?

3 Verse 5 says that Jesus 'saw their faith'. How did the man's friends show their faith?

ICT MI

Through the Roof is a Christian organisation that works with disabled and non-disabled people to make the message of Jesus accessible and help people reach their full potential in God. They take their name from the story in **Mark 2:1-12**.

Through the roof

Making the Christian message accessible

1 Visit their website www.throughtheroof.org to find out about their work.

2 Design a poster for Through the Roof.

• Create a new logo based on their name, or the story in **Mark 2:1-12**

• Include information about the work of Through the Roof.

TPD SM

Think about the facilities that cater for the disabled pupils in your school and local community. For example:

• How many sets of stairs are in your school?

• How many lifts are there?

• Are there buttons for automatically opening doors?

• Are there wheelchair ramps?

• Are there any special computers for use by blind or partially sighted pupils?

Com

If there is a wheelchair user or blind or partially sighted person in your class, why not ask them to talk the class about how they cope with getting around the school?

How do people with Special Needs face Discrimination?

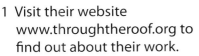

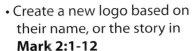

If people with special needs are not offered the same opportunities and facilities as other people, it is a form of **discrimination**. People can feel isolated and alone because of being treated in such a way.

Sometimes people don't even realise the difficulties faced by those with special needs. It is only when we try to put ourselves in someone else's position that we can understand the problems and obstacles they might face during the day.

MI WO

What difficulties might someone partially sighted or using a wheelchair encounter leading a normal school life?

• In **pairs**, take a walk round your school following one day's timetable. Make a list of any difficulties you would have including stairs, crowded corridors, moving around the classroom, reading, writing and anything else you encounter.

• For each difficulty you encountered, suggest a possible solution.

Com
TPD
WO

Get into **pairs** for the following activity. It should help you to understand what life can be like for somebody who is partially sighted.

- One person should wear a blindfold.

- The other person should direct their partner round the classroom by only using verbal instructions.

- Only one pair should do this at a time. Your teacher doesn't want any accidents.

- When every pair has had a turn, discuss the experience as a class.
  - What was it like to not be able to see?
  - Was it difficult having to trust somebody else's commands?
  - How would you cope if you were never able to see again?

ICT
MI
SM

Research

Joni Eareckson Tada was left **quadriplegic** (paralysed from the neck down) after a diving accident in 1967. She was only 17 years old and had been healthy and athletic before the accident. She is a Christian author, artist and founder of the organisation **Joni and Friends**.

Use the internet or a library to find out as much as you can about Joni.

- What happened to Joni after her accident?

- What does Joni have to say about her disability now? Is she angry? Sad? Accepting?

- Is she married?

- What work does the organisation Joni and Friends do?

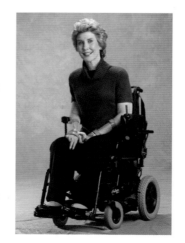

Used with permission of Joni and Friends.

The Disability Discrimination Act

In 1995 the government passed the **Disability Discrimination Act** (**DDA**), which aimed to end the prejudice and mistreatment faced by many disabled people. This act gives disabled people rights in the areas of:

- Employment.

- Education.

- Buying or renting land or property, including making it easier for tenants to adapt their premises to suit their disability.

Disability in School

While most schools are very supportive of all of their pupils, some parents feel that their children have been discriminated against because they have special needs. Read about the experiences of two pupils, Lisa and Jack.

Lisa's story

Janice Dunlop believes that her daughter Lisa, who is 14 years old and uses a wheelchair, has suffered discrimination because of her disability. Lisa was refused entry to her local school, which is just over a mile from their home. Janice believes that the school was too concerned about getting good examination results to bother helping pupils with physical disabilities.

'Lisa did eventually get a place in the school,' Janice says, 'but we feel that they would rather she wasn't there.'

Lisa's problems are not just confined to the classroom. 'It's not only in lessons that Lisa should be with her peers, but at after school activities as well. The school doesn't organise any trips that a child in a wheelchair can go on. She puts on a brave face but I know she is hurt.'

Jack's Story

Jack is a Year 11 pupil and is partially blind. Unable to read the board, Jack quickly started to fall behind. His parents asked the school to help.

The school said that they couldn't put his needs above those of others in his class. The school did not have a lot of money to spare, so Jack simply did not receive the support he required.

Jack had to move to a school fifteen miles away. His mother said, 'Parents want their child to be included in the local community. They want them to meet children who live up the street and to be invited to their birthday parties. If you live in one town but go to school in another, it's not easy to make friends locally.'

Jack is now happily settled at a school which caters well for children with special needs. In fact, he loves it. He has a classroom assistant, Mrs Kennedy, who helps him by writing down the words if he cannot see the board. 'I like Maths, French and PE, but Art is my best subject. It's something that other people say that I'm good at. I get all the help I need.'

BC TPD SM
Imagine that you are **Lisa** or **Jack**. Write a series of diary entries describing your experiences at school.

TPD SM
Both Lisa and Jack come from Christian families. How could their local churches and Christian friends help them to cope with their school experiences?

Com TPD WO
Read the statements below:

'School is not only about exams. It's about creating people who are tolerant and willing to include everyone.'

'People with special needs should be taught in whatever school they want to go to.'

In groups of three, discuss whether you agree with each of these statements.

Are there any potential problems with these views?

Organisations

There are many different charities and organisations which support people who are blind, deaf, suffering from paralysis or other disabilities. Most of these organisations are not supported financially by the government. They survive on donations and the goodwill of volunteer workers.

Here are some examples:

- **National Deaf Children's Society** is dedicated to creating a 'world without barriers' for deaf children and young people. It provides a Freephone Helpline, specialist advisers on all aspects of childhood deafness and events for families and children.

Guide Dogs

• **The Guide Dogs For The Blind Association** provides dogs to help blind and partially sighted people. It is supported by volunteer breeders and puppy walkers who train the dogs to guide those who can't see. The association also funds research projects to find further cures for eye disease.

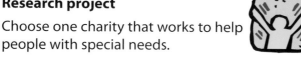

The voice of learning disability

• **Mencap** is a charity in the UK which helps and supports people with mental disabilities and their families. Amongst other services, it trains those with learning difficulties to find jobs and to live more independently.

Com
ICT
MI
SM

Research project

Choose one charity that works to help people with special needs.

Use the internet or library to find out the following information:

• When it was founded.

• Where it is based.

• Who it helps.

• What it does to help.

• How you and your classmates could help this charity.

Make a presentation to the class about your chosen charity. Your presentation should last approximately **three minutes**.

The Special Olympics

The **Special Olympics** is an international, non-profit organisation dedicated to helping and empowering those with learning disabilities. It provides year-round sports training and campaigns against prejudice towards disabled people. Famously, the organisation also holds an international sporting competition every four years. More than one hundred and eighty countries compete. The Special Olympics Summer Games started in 1968. Winter games followed in 1977.

The Special Olympics helps over two and a half million children and adults in various important ways. They offer those with learning disabilities the opportunities to:

• realise their full potential.

• become more self-confident.

• befriend other athletes.

• be proud of their achievements.

• develop physical fitness.

In 2003 the eleventh Special Olympics World Summer Games were held in Dublin, Ireland. This was the first time the event took place outside the United States.

ICT

Find out more about the Special Olympics and what the organisation does by visiting their website at **www.specialolympics.org**.

MI
BC
TPD
SM

Design a poster celebrating the Special Olympics. You will need:

• A **logo**. You can use the actual Special Olympics one or design your own.

• A **slogan**. This should be short and catchy.

• Some attractive **images**.

Com
MI
BC
SM

Pretend you are a newspaper reporter at the 2008 Paralympics in Beijing. Write an article describing the event.

• Find out the different ways that physically disabled athletes can compete in sport.

• Give your article a catchy headline.

• Describe some of the different events.

• Illustrate your report with a drawing or a photograph.

The Paralympics

The **Paralympics** is an international multi-sport event for competitors with a range of physical disabilities. It takes place every four years following the Olympic Games.

The summer event features sports such as archery, cycling, judo, rowing and volleyball, while the winter games features skiing, ice hockey and curling.

The Paralympics has been staged in countries such as Japan, Canada, Spain and Greece. In 2008, it was held in Beijing.

Careers, Work and Unemployment

When you are at school your future career might seem a very long way off, but since you were a small child people have probably been asking you 'What would you like to do when you grow up?' Some people are very sure what work they would like to do, while others have no idea.

As you get older, people will talk to you more and more about what job you would like to do. You will most likely attend careers classes in school. People take their choice of career very seriously, particularly if they will be doing that job for the rest of their lives.

Com WO EfE PD	Discuss these questions with a partner:

Discuss these questions with a partner:

As a young child, how did you reply when people asked what you wanted to do when you grow up?

Why did you give that answer?

How would you answer the question now?

MI SM	Make a list of all the different kinds

Make a list of all the different kinds of 'work' you do every week. It can include school work, cleaning and tidying, cooking, dog walking and anything you do that is productive.

Look at the list. Which tasks do you enjoy most?

Why work?

Human beings are natural workers. Whether studying hard at school, practising to improve sporting skills, or concentrating on developing our friendships, we will always try to spend our time doing something useful.

There is a great feeling of satisfaction in doing a job and doing it well. Setting yourself a goal and accomplishing it can be very rewarding, particularly if you are doing something that benefits others in some way.

The Bible teaches that God has a very positive view of work. God is a worker and work is important in the lives of Christians.

In the book of Genesis we read about the first people, instructed by God to work in and care for the world around them (**Genesis 1:28**). Work is part of God's good creation. God expects people to work to provide for their families and to be generous to others.

Christians believe that they can give glory to God and be an example for him by working hard in their jobs. **1 Thessalonians 4:11-12** says;

> 'Make it your ambition to lead a quiet life, to mind your own business and to work with your hands, just as we told you, so that your daily life may win the respect of outsiders and so that you will not be dependent on anybody.'

By maintaining a good attitude and good discipline, Christians can serve God faithfully wherever they are.

There are several other reasons for working hard.

1 **To make money**.

We need money to buy food, clothes, a place to live, and to pay the monthly bills. We also need money to fund our leisure activities and luxuries such as eating out in restaurants or going on holidays.

2 **To socialise with others**.

Once you have left school, work is one of the main ways to meet others and make close friends.

3 **To feel good**.

Do you ever feel a sense of achievement when you do particularly well in sports or in school? We all feel good when we are successful at something. We can also experience this at work. **Proverbs 13:4** teaches:

> ' The sluggard craves and gets nothing, but the desires of the diligent are fully satisfied.'

4 **To organise our day**.

Work provides us with a daily routine, gives us a sense of purpose and prevents boredom.

5 **To be creative**.

Many people choose a particular job because it allows them to use their skills. For example, artists, writers, musicians and even teachers all use their creative abilities in their jobs.

Ma MI TPD WO EfE

1 In **pairs**, discuss the reasons for working listed above. Put them in order of importance. Compare your order with other groups.

Make a pie chart showing what reasons the class consider most important.

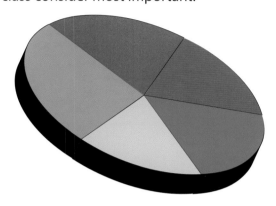

2 Can you think of any other reasons why people work? Try to come up with at least **three** more.

Sometimes work doesn't seem like a good idea, especially if you have ever delivered a paper round in the rain, or spent a summer working on a farm, digging in the hot sun. Although we try to find work that we enjoy, some parts will always be difficult.

Com BC SM

Have you ever done a job you really didn't enjoy? Write a couple of paragraphs explaining what your job involved and describing what was so unpleasant about it.

The Bible gives an interesting view on doing jobs we don't enjoy. It teaches Christians that they are really working for God.

> 'Whatever you do, work at it with all your heart, as working for the Lord, not for men, since you know you will receive an inheritance from the Lord as a reward. It is the Lord Christ you are serving.'
>
> (**Colossians 3:23-24**)

MI
TPD
SM

How do you think the words of **Colossians 3:23-24** would bring comfort to someone working hard in a job they didn't enjoy?

Hard Work Pays Off

Sarah had worked hard for her exams this time. At Christmas she had been so disappointed with her results. She could still picture the moment when her parents had opened her report. 'Sarah needs to work much harder', her teacher had written. They were the worst results she had ever had.

'I'm not coming out this weekend.' Sarah said. 'I have to study.'

'I don't know why you're so worried,' moaned Jane. 'We're only in Year 10! It's not as if they're important exams.'

Jane seemed to do very little work in school and yet still did all right in exams. Recently, she had started to skip some classes and borrow Sarah's book to copy up. Once, she forgot to bring the book back, getting Sarah into trouble with the teacher.

The bell rang. Last period Friday meant PE, so the girls dashed up the corridor, dumped their bags in the cloakrooms and ran into the sports hall. They were having a special aerobics

teacher today so they were keen to get there on time. The class was so enjoyable that everyone forgot, for an hour at least, that their exams were starting on Monday.

The cloakrooms buzzed with talk about exam week; 'All the best', 'Don't work too hard'. Sarah smiled to herself. She *had* worked hard. She was ready for the exams this time. All she needed to do this weekend was spend a few hours revising History for the exam on Monday.

Sarah put on her coat and lifted her bag. It was open. The contents spilled out onto the ground. She looked puzzled. She was always careful to close her bag. Sarah bent down to pick up her belongings. 'Wait a minute,' she thought, 'where's my History file?' She searched the cloakroom frantically. It wasn't there! People were starting to drift home. What would she do?

By this time Jane was sitting on the bus. 'Sarah won't miss this file,' she thought. 'She has all her revision done and was at all the classes. I'll slip it back in her bag on Monday. Wow, I've saved myself a lot of work.'

MI
BC
TPD
PD

1 Describe both Sarah and Jane's attitudes towards their schoolwork.

2 If you were in Jane's position, would you have taken Sarah's file? Be honest.

3 If you were in Sarah's position, what would you do if you found out that Jane had taken your file without asking?

4 How would you like the story to end? Write an ending explaining what happens next.
 • Does Sarah's hard work pay off?
 • What happens to Jane?
 • Do the girls remain friends?

Skills and Gifts

The Bible teaches that each person's unique talents are gifts from God. In **Romans 12:6-8**, Paul writes:

> 'We have different gifts, according to the grace given us. If a man's gift is prophesying, let him use it in proportion to his faith. If it is serving, let him serve; if it is teaching, let him teach; if it is encouraging, let him encourage; if it is contributing to the needs of others, let him give generously; if it is leadership, let him govern diligently; if it is showing mercy, let him do it cheerfully.'

Everyone has different skills and abilities. One person in your class might be very good at sport, but that is not to say that they are a talented artist as well. Likewise, someone else might be a brilliant musician but they might not be as good in science.

In the book of Exodus, Bezalel was specially gifted by God to be an excellent artist and craftsman.

> 'Then Moses said to the Israelites, "See, the Lord has chosen Bezalel son of Uri, the son of Hur, of the tribe of Judah, and he has filled him with the Spirit of God, with skill, ability and knowledge in all kinds of crafts- to make artistic designs for work in gold, silver and bronze, to cut and set stones, to work in wood and to engage in all kinds of artistic craftsmanship.'

(Exodus 35:30-33)

When choosing a career it is important to take into account the things that you are naturally good at.

Com
TPD

'Find something you love to do and you'll never have to work a day in your life.'

What do you think this saying means? Discuss your thoughts with a partner.

Com
TPD
WO

Get into groups of **four** and follow the instructions.

1 Take a few moments to consider your own gifts.
   - What are you good at?
   - What do you love doing?
   - Why do you love doing it?

2 Taking turns, each person in the group should take a minute to tell the others about their gifts and abilities.
   - How are you gifted?
   - When did you first notice that you were talented in this area?
   - Did you inherit it from anyone in your family?
   - How can your gift be used to benefit others?

Hopefully, there were a few different gifts in your group. This exercise should prove that each of us has their own talents, and each has the potential to help others.

Sometimes we can be unsure what our own gifts or talents are. We might be modest, or think the things that we do are nothing special.

Sometimes it can be helpful to have someone who knows us well tell us what we're good at. Likewise, it can be helpful if you remind your own friends the things that they're good at.

Vocation

The word **vocation** refers to a career which someone feels specially drawn to. More than simply being interested, vocation is a gut feeling that you want to spend your life doing this particular job. Some people might describe a nursing, teaching or social work job as their vocation.

The word vocation literally means 'calling', and it comes from the Christian tradition of people feeling called by God to a specific task.

MI
SM

There are many stories in the Bible of people being chosen by God to perform a particular task. Here are some examples:

- Abraham (**Genesis 12:1-9**)
- Moses (**Exodus 3**)
- Jonah (**Jonah 1-3**)
- Noah (**Genesis 6-8**)
- Saul (**Acts 9:1-31**)
- Samuel (**1 Samuel 3**)
- Jeremiah (**Jeremiah 1:4-19**)
- Mary and Joseph (**Matthew 1:18-24** and **Luke 1:26-38**)

Look up each of the passages and answer the following questions for each:

1 Where was this person when they were called?
2 What age were they?
3 How did God call this person?
4 How did they respond?
5 What did they do next?

Many Christians today describe a sense that God is calling them to one particular area of work. This does not normally mean that they hear God speaking aloud to them, as Moses did at the burning bush. Rather, they feel guided that they should make certain decisions or steer their life in a particular direction.

The word vocation is still most frequently used when describing the call to be a priest, minister or missionary, but Christians do not restrict the idea of God's calling to church jobs. Christians believe that God has a unique plan for the life of each individual that includes using their gifts, skills and abilities.

Com
TPD
EfE

Have you ever felt that you should be doing a particular job? Perhaps you have felt a strong desire to help with a youth group or volunteer with an organisation?

Discuss your thoughts with a partner.

MI
TPD

Do you know anyone whose job could be considered a vocation?

Making a decision

When choosing a career it is important to make sure that your choice is the right one. Pay and holidays may be important to some people, while others might be more concerned with how interesting the job is. After all, if you are going to spend most of your life working you will want to do something that you enjoy.

TPD
PD
EfE

Which would you prefer: A job that you don't like but pays a lot **or** a job that doesn't pay so well, but you love doing?

'I love food! pasta, chips, burgers, curry, Chinese food, Indian food, cakes and desserts! I'm going to be a world famous chef and make lots of money with my chain of restaurants!'

Some people say that they have always known which career path they should follow. They say that from a very early age they wanted to work in a particular job when they grew up.

For others, their choice of career was not so obvious but they are still happy in their job. For example, **Noreen** has been nursing for over 25 years. She enjoys her job and manages to balance a career with her family life.

'I don't feel I was called by God to be a nurse in the sense that one day I heard a voice telling me to do this job. But as a Christian I do feel content that I am where God wants me to be. I get a great sense of fulfilment in helping others to get better and being with them to help them in their suffering. Nursing is hard work and it takes time and patience to learn some of the skills needed to be a good nurse. But I'm very happy in my career and would recommend it to anyone.'

MI
TPD
SM

Sam comes from a family that is involved in full-time Christian work. His sister is a missionary, his brother is a Presbyterian minister and his parents, though now retired, had been RE teachers. Sam studied art at university and is a talented painter, but he felt that an art-related career wasn't an appropriate way to serve God. He currently works as a computer programmer for a large Christian charity. He does enjoy parts of his job and he is happy to be involved in Christian work of some kind, but he longs to be using his creative talents.

1 Has Sam made the right career choice?

2 What advice would you give Sam in his situation?

3 How could you use the Bible to help Sam? Try referring to the passages listed on the opposite page.

MI
TPD
SM
PD
EfE

Some of the things that people consider when choosing a career are outlined in the chart below. Draw a similar chart, listing **five** things that you think will be important to you when it is time to choose your career.

- How much will I get paid?
- How interesting will the work be?
- What will my parents think?
- CHOOSING A CAREER
- Will others see me as important?
- Will my work help others?
- Is the work outside or in an office?
- What holidays will I get?
- Is this what God wants me to do?

Unemployment

When a person does not have a job, they are described as being **unemployed**. This can happen for a number of different reasons, many of which are out of that person's control.

1. Business can slow down. For example, if there is no need for new housing then many builders may be out of work.

2. People can be replaced by technology. In some cases it is cheaper to build a machine to do a job then pay a person to do it.

3. Illness may stop people from working. If someone is ill or injured for a long time they may have no choice but to leave work.

4. Some people find it hard to get qualifications, especially if they did not study hard at school. Many people could apply for the same post, and the job will be given to the person with the best qualifications. Depending on the job, employers may look for GCSEs, A-levels, GNVQs, university degrees or more.

MI · TPD · SM · Cit

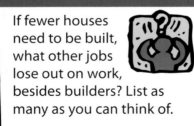

If fewer houses need to be built, what other jobs lose out on work, besides builders? List as many as you can think of.

Being unemployed can be very difficult. People find themselves without money, which is particularly worrying for those with families to feed. Not being out at work can leave people lonely, without structure to their day, with no goals to achieve or challenges to meet. This can even lead to stress and depression.

In this country people can apply for a **Job Seeker's Allowance**- money that the government gives to those who are unemployed. It is usually only a very small amount, maybe just enough to buy food.

ICT · MI · SM · Cit

The idea that the government should give money to those who are unemployed was suggested by **William Beveridge**.

He also suggested that the government should provide free education and free health care. Previously, you would have paid a lot of money to go to school or visit the doctor.

Use the internet or a library to research William Beveridge and his ideas.

- When did he live?
- Why did he come up with his ideas?

We read in the New Testament that some people were unemployed, not because they were unable to find work, but because they were unwilling to work. Paul has some strong words for them.

> 'We hear that some among you are idle. They are not busy; they are busybodies. Such people we command and urge in the Lord Jesus Christ to settle down and earn the bread they eat.'
>
> (**2 Thessalonians 3:11-12**)

Likewise, there are some people today who think it is acceptable to do no work, even when they are capable. In this case, government money that could be given to people who are sick, or to people who are trying hard to find work, is being taken by those who have decided not to work for themselves. The Bible warns against laziness and teaches that it is good to work.

> 'He who has been stealing must steal no longer, but must work, doing something useful with his own hands, that he may have something to share with those in need.'
>
> (**Ephesians 4:28**)

MI
TPD
SM

There are lots of ways people can stay productive while trying to find steady work. Copy out the table and put each activity in the box which you think suits it best.

What work can the unemployed do?

Help yourself	Help your family	Help society

home improvement   gardening
knitting   growing vegetables
youth club   child-minding
collecting for charity   dog-walking
computer classes   an education course
painting   charity shop work
school committee   sports
helping the elderly   reading
cleaning   hospital visits

Unemployment can bring a lot of worry about the future, but understanding the Christian view can help people to cope. The Bible teaches that it is important to see things as completely under God's rule and control.

MI
TPD

Read **Jeremiah 29:11**.

Explain how this verse could give encouragement to someone who finds themselves unemployed.

The important things in life

Society places great importance on what we do for a living. Often, the first question you are asked when you meet someone is 'What do you do?'

We must remember that work is not the most important thing in life. Some people's jobs are

valuable causes that they can devote their lives to, while others work quite happily in any job to provide for their family.

MI
TPD
WO
PD

What are the most important things in your life? Family? Friends?

Make a list of the 5 most important things.

Compare your list with a partner. What are the similarities and differences?

We are sometimes told that we ought to be judged by how powerful we are, how much money we earn or what kind of car we drive. We can feel as though our ultimate goal in life is to make as much money as possible or to have the best house or the nicest clothes.

The Bible gives us a blunt reminder when it teaches that even the greatest achievements in life will mean nothing when we die.

'Do not be overawed when a man grows rich,

when the splendour of his house increases;

for he will take nothing with him when he dies,

his splendour will not descend with him.'

(Psalm 49:16-17)

Christians believe that we cannot measure our value by what we do or how much we own, but only by what God thinks of us. The Bible teaches that no matter what job somebody does, or whether they have one, they are loved by God. Each human being is created by God in his image. They are valuable and significant.

Money

Christians believe that all good things come from God and that he provides people with the things that they need to live a happy, fulfilling life. **Psalm 24:1** says:

> 'The earth is the Lord's, and everything in it, the world, and all who live in it; for he founded it upon the seas and established it upon the waters.'

This includes money. The Bible teaches that God gives people good things for their benefit, and also so they can benefit others. He wants people to use what he has given them wisely. Christians aim to use their money in ways that honour God and help others.

TPD
SM

Before you read the rest of this chapter, quickly make a list of the ways in which you could use your money to help other people.

Com
TPD
WO

'**Money makes the world go round**' is a famous saying.

What do you think it means?

Do you think it is true?

Discuss your thoughts with a partner.

Attitudes to money

You may have heard people say '**Money is the root of all evil**'. This is perhaps the most misquoted verse in the Bible. We can find the actual teaching in **1 Timothy 6:7-10**.

'For we brought nothing into the world, and we can take nothing out of it. But if we have food and clothing we will be content with that. People who want to get rich fall into temptation and a trap and into many foolish and harmful desires that plunge men into ruin and destruction. For the love of money is a root of all kinds of evil. Some people, eager for money, have wandered from the faith and pierced themselves with many sorrows.'

The Bible teaches that it is not money itself which is dangerous, but the love of money. Christians believe that if we place too much importance on gaining wealth we risk replacing God, family and friends as the most important things in our lives. People experience problems when they lose track of what is important in life and begin to love money too much.

MI
TPD
SM

Read **1 Timothy 6:7-10** again and answer the following questions.

1 What is meant by 'For we have brought nothing into the world, and we can take nothing out of it'? Explain it in your own words.

2 What kind of 'trap' could people fall into if getting rich became the most important thing in their life?

3 Can you think of any examples of how love of money can cause someone 'many sorrows'?

Have you ever been given the impression that getting rich was the ultimate goal in life?

Can you think of any problems that would arise if getting rich was your only interest?

The English novelist Henry Fielding wrote;

'Make money your god and it will plague you like the devil.'

As a class, discuss what you think he meant by this statement.

One character in the Bible who struggled with the love of money was **The Rich Young Man**. We read about him in **Matthew 19:16-30**. He approaches Jesus asking what he should do to inherit eternal life. Jesus tells him, 'Sell your possessions and give to the poor, and you will have treasure in heaven. Then come, follow me.'

The rich young man finds it too difficult to put Jesus' message into practice. We read that, 'he went away sad'. He wants to follow Jesus, yet he is not willing to give up his great wealth as Jesus asks. This passage clearly shows the power that money can have over people.

Read **Matthew 19:16-30**, then answer the following questions.

1 Why do you think Jesus asks the rich young man to give away all of his money and possessions?

2 What do you think Jesus means when he describes a camel going through the eye of a needle?

3 What do you think Jesus means when he says, 'Many who are first will be last, and many who are last will be first.'

Greed

The Bible clearly warns against greed of all kinds. In fact, the last of the Ten Commandments (**Exodus 20:17**) speaks of the sin of **coveting** your neighbour's possessions. To **covet** means to desire something strongly, particularly those things which belong to somebody else.

Can you think of any occasions when you were jealous of a friend's birthday or Christmas presents? Perhaps they were given a toy you really wanted, or some expensive clothes that you could not afford.

The Bible teaches that some people are never satisfied with what they own or have, so they long for more.

'Whoever loves money never has money enough; whoever loves wealth is never satisfied with his income.'

(**Ecclesiastes 5:10**)

It is important to develop a balanced attitude towards money. In **Matthew 6:19-21**, Jesus reminds people that wealth does not last.

'Do not store up for yourselves treasures on earth, where moth and rust destroy, and where thieves break in and steal. But store up for yourselves treasures in heaven, where moth and rust do not destroy, and where thieves do not break in and steal. For where your treasure is, there your heart will be also.'

A **treasure** is something that has great worth. It might have great financial value. The rich young man, for example, treasured his money and possessions, so much so that he was not willing to part with them.

A treasure might also be something that has emotional importance or is special to you. This might be a piece of jewellery which you inherited from a relative, or a toy that you have had since you were a small child.

Whatever form your treasure takes, you would be devastated if it was broken, lost or stolen.

Com	Read **Matthew 6:19-21** again and answer the following questions **in pairs**.
MI	
TPD	
WO	

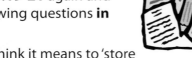

1 What do you think it means to 'store up treasures on earth'?

2 What do you think Jesus means by 'treasures in heaven'?

3 Why do you think wealth and possessions are so important to us?

4 What do you think the phrase 'where your treasure is, there your heart will be also' means? Come up with your own saying explaining the same message.

5 Take a few minutes to discuss the things which you treasure. If you had to leave your home, and were only allowed to bring **five** possessions, which ones would you take? Explain your choices.

Using money wisely

The Bible teaches that people should take responsibility for what they do with what God has given them. This includes using money wisely. **1 Corinthians 4:2** says:

'Now it is required that those who have been given a trust must prove faithful.'

By saving carefully and investing wisely, we might be able to make more money, which we can use to provide for our families or to help others. Nowhere is this teaching more clear than in the **Parable of the Talents**.

The Parable of the Talents

A rich landowner was about to take a long trip so he gathered his most trusted servants around him to give them instructions. He told them that he was going to give each of them a certain amount of money to invest while he was gone. The money, called **talents**, was worth about one thousand pounds each. The master gave:

- **five talents** to the **first servant**;
- **two talents** to the **second servant**;
- **one talent** to the **third servant**.

Each servant was given the appropriate amount of talents according to their individual abilities. What an enormous amount of money each of them had!

Both the first servant and the second servant invested their talents wisely. Each doubled their master's money. But the third servant saw no point in trying to make a profit for his master at the risk of losing the money altogether. He foolishly dug a large hole in the ground and buried the money inside.

When the master returned, the first two servants brought the money to him and described how they increased his wealth. The master was delighted, and complimented their faithful and responsible actions. He rewarded them with honour and even greater responsibility. But the third servant faced his master and admitted that he had done nothing with the one talent given to him.

The master was furious! His reaction to the third servant was disappointment and punishment. He took the money away from the foolish servant

and gave it to the man who had ten talents. The foolish servant was then thrown out of the house.

The master declared,

'For everyone who has will be given more, and he will have an abundance. Whoever does not have, even what he was will be taken from him.'

(**Matthew 25:29**)

MI
SM

Use the Bible references to answer the questions.

1 How many talents were the three servants given? (**Matthew 25:15**)

2 What did the servant with five talents and the servant with two talents do with the master's money? (**Matthew 25:16-17**)

3 What did the servant with one talent do with the master's money? (**Matthew 25:18**)

4 Which of the servants pleased their master? (**Matthew 25:20-23**)

---

5 What reward was given to them? (**Matthew 25:21, 23**)

6 What punishment did the master give to the unfaithful servant? (**Matthew 25:30**)

MI
BC
WO

Read **Matthew 25:14-30** as a class.

In groups, create and perform a short roleplay or script based on the passage.

• One person should act as a narrator while the others should act out the story.

• You could write lines for the characters or perform it as a mime.

Jesus told the Parable of the Talents to show the importance of using what God has given us wisely, including money. Christians should not waste their money by overspending on things that they do not need, but they should also not keep their money hidden away and do nothing with it.

MI
TPD
SM

Match the definition in the right column to the word in the left.

Word	Definition
Steward	Loyalty to God and a strong belief in him.
Stewardship	Someone who manages what God has given him.
Talent	Money given in support of the Church.
God	Something of great value and importance.
Offering	Creator and owner of all things.
Faithful	A God-given ability
Treasure	Using time, abilities and money wisely.

Poverty

Poverty means not being able to provide for basic material needs. This can mean being unable to access food, clothing, housing, toilets and washing facilities, education and health care.

Absolute poverty means living on less than one US dollar per day.

- 10% of the world's population live on less than $1 per day.
- 50% of the world's population live on less than $2.50 per day.

(source: World Bank Development Indicators 2008)

WO
Cit

Do you think of yourself as rich? Where would you place yourself on this scale of the poorest and richest people in the world?

Poorest   **Richest**

Stand Up, Sit Down

Play this game as a class. One person reads out the following instructions:

- Stand up if your house has a floor.
- Sit down if your house doesn't have running water.
- Stay standing if anyone in your family has ever owned a car.
- Sit down if you have never had a TV at home.
- Stay standing if you have ever had a computer at home.

If you are still standing at the end of the game, then you are one of the richest 2% of people in the world.

- How did you find this exercise?
- Do you consider yourself rich?
- Do you find it hard to believe that you are one of the richest 2% in the world?

Even though we are very rich compared to some other countries, people here can still find it hard to afford what they need.

In 2003, a report stated that **one in three** children in Northern Ireland lives in 'relative poverty'.

This means some people don't have very much money compared to most of the country. It may be hard to provide for basic needs like food, or decent housing.

TPD
Cit

Why are some people rich, while others are poor?

Make a list of as many possible reasons as you can think of.

In the Bible, there are over 2,000 passages showing God's concern for people who are living in poverty.

> 'He who oppresses the poor shows contempt for their Maker, but whoever is kind to the needy honours God.'
>
> **(Proverbs 14:31)**

> 'If anyone has material possessions and sees his brother in need but has no pity on him, how can the love of God be in him? Dear children, let us not love with words or tongue but with actions and in truth.'
>
> **(1 John 3:17-18)**

MI
TPD
The book of Amos has some strong words for people who were worshipping God, but treating the poor badly. Look up the verses and answer the questions.

1 **Amos 4:1**.   Here we read of some women who were living very comfortably, while mistreating the poor.

What animal does God compare them to?

2 **Amos 5:11-12**.   How were people treating the poor?

3 **Amos 5:21-24**.   What does God says he hates?

Why might people find that unusual?

Why might God be saying this?

What does God say he wants?

Statistics

Have a look at how the world spends its money every year.

The figures are in US billions. That's a '1' and nine '0's (1,000,000,000).

- Amount spent on hair and makeup in the USA: $8 Billion
- Amount spent on ice cream in Europe: $11 Billion
- Amount spent on pet foods in Europe and the USA: $17 Billion
- Amount spent on cigarettes in Europe: $50 Billion
- Amount spent on alcohol in Europe: $105 Billion

Compare this to the amount of money it would cost to end poverty the world over:

- Amount required to provide basic education for all: $6 Billion
- Amount required to provide clean water for all: $9 Billion
- Amount required to provide basic health care for all: $13 Billion

Source: globalissues.org (Figures from 1998)

Ma
MI
Cit
Look at the statistics above.

1 How much money do we spend on ice cream?

2 How much money would it cost to give every child in the world an education?

3 If we stopped buying cigarettes and used the money to provide education, clean water and basic health care for everyone in the world, how much money would we have left over?

TPD
SM
Cit
How do the statistics above make you feel?

Can you think of anything that could be done to encourage people to spend their money more responsibly?

Fairtrade

The way you spend your money has tremendous power to affect the lives of people in other parts of the world.

Have you ever thought about where the things you buy come from, and who put in the hard work so you can have them?

Many of the products we enjoy (such as cocoa, tea, coffee and many types of fruit) are grown in Africa, Asia or Latin America by farmers who earn little for their hard work. Sadly, unfair trade rules and the power of big companies often means that farmers earn less money than it costs them to grow their products. This keeps them in poverty and means they are unable to invest in their future.

Fairtrade ensures farmers earn a decent living. By choosing products with the FAIRTRADE Mark you can ensure that your money is helping people to work their way out of poverty, rather than keeping them there.

Find out more at **www.fairtrade.org.uk**.

Giving

'**Not he who has much is rich, but he who gives much.**'

Erich Fromm

Ma
MI
SM

Imagine for a moment that a wealthy relative gives you **one million pounds**. That's **one '1'** and **six '0's**.

£1,000,000

Exciting, isn't it? But there's one small condition: you can't save any of it – you have to spend or give away the whole lot. Every single penny.

Using a calculator, copy and complete the following table deciding how much you would spend on each item.

You can spend as much or as little as you like for each one, as long as you don't exceed **one million pounds**. Be honest!

Item	Amount (£)
Clothes	
A new house	
Parents	
Cars	
Food	
Friends	
Holidays	
Brothers and Sisters	
DVDs	
Charity	
Parties	
Jewellery	
Church	
Music	
Video games	
Beauty Products	

Copy the table below and add up how much you spent on yourself, your family and others.

Person	Amount
Yourself	
Family	
Others	

Look over your results and answer the following questions.

1 Are you surprised by the results?

2 What do you think they reveal about you?
   • Would you say that you are a greedy person?
   • Would you say that you are a generous person?

3 Do you think it is important to share your wealth with others?
   • Your family?
   • Your friends?
   • People you don't know?

The Bible is full of references to looking after others. When Jesus talked about wealth he taught that people have a duty to care for one another, particularly those who are poor and needy.

> 'For I was hungry and you gave me something to eat, I was thirsty and you gave me something to drink, I was a stranger and you invited me in, I needed clothes and you clothed me, I was sick and you looked after me, I was in prison and you came to visit me.'
>
> (**Matthew 25:35-36**)

You do not have to own or give away a million pounds to be able to help other people. The Bible teaches that God is delighted whenever somebody displays generosity to another human being.

> 'Suppose a brother or sister is without clothes and daily food. If one of you says to him, 'Go, I wish you well; keep warm and well fed,' but does nothing about his physical needs, what good is it? In the same way, faith by itself, if it is not accompanied by action, it is dead.'
>
> (**James 2:15-17**)

Clearly, it is very important to give to those in need. It is not enough to pray for the homeless and the starving. Practical help is also needed. This charitable attitude was an important feature of the early church mentioned in the book of Acts.

> 'All the believers were together and had everything in common. Selling their possessions and goods, they gave to anyone as he had need.'
>
> (**Acts 2:44-45**)

MI
TPD

Read **Acts 2:44-47**.

Why do you think these first Christians had everyone's respect?

Do you know of any churches today who live like the church in Acts?

What would the world be like if every church tried to live this way?

Jesus taught that giving should come from the heart. **2 Corinthians 9:7** tells us that 'God loves a cheerful giver'. When giving money, we should do so willingly because we should want to help others, not reluctantly because we are told to do so.

Jesus also encouraged his followers to think about the reasons why they gave money to charity. Many people at that time gave in order to receive praise from others. Jesus labelled these people **hypocrites** – people who pretend to be something they are not. In **Matthew 6:1-4**, Jesus was critical of those who show off whilst giving away their money:

> 'Be careful not to do your 'acts of righteousness' before men, to be seen by them. If you do, you will have no reward from your Father in heaven. So when you give to the needy, do not announce it with trumpets, as the hypocrites do in the synagogues and on the streets, to be honoured by men. I tell you the truth, they have received their reward in full. But when you give to the needy, do not let your left hand know what your right hand is doing, so that your giving may be in secret. Then your father, who sees what is done in secret, will reward you.'

Some people had claimed that they were performing 'acts of righteousness', but they were not donating money to be help others. They wanted to make themselves look good. Rather than giving in a private, humble way, they made sure that other

people could see what they were doing. Jesus said that whatever praise these hypocrites received from people would be their only reward.

The message here is clear: we should not draw attention to ourselves, but give quietly. Only God should know how much has been given.

MI SM

Read **Matthew 6:1-4** carefully and answer the following questions.

1 Jesus says, 'Do not let your left hand know what your right hand is doing.' This is an unusual statement. What do you think it means?

2 What kind of reward do you think Jesus is talking about in verse 4?

Com BC TPD

Mother Teresa famously said;

'Let us not be satisfied with just giving money. Money is not enough, money can be got, but they need your hearts to love them. So, spread your love everywhere you go.'

Try rewriting this instruction in your own words.

BC TPD WO

Get into **groups** of **four or five**. Design and draw a poster illustrating all of the practical ways in which we can help others.

In **Luke 21:1-4**, we read about an occasion when one poor woman's generous giving was compared to the actions of the rich hypocrites.

'As he looked up, Jesus saw the rich putting their gifts into the temple treasury. He also saw a poor widow put in two very small copper coins. 'I tell you the truth,' he said, 'this poor widow has put in more than all the others. All these people gave their gifts out of their wealth; but she out of her poverty put in all she had to live on.''

Some people might have turned their noses up at the small amount of money that the poor widow put into the collection, especially compared with that which other people were giving. However, although she might have only given two coins, this was all the money that she had to give. Whereas others only gave a small fraction of their wealth, this woman gave everything.

Gambling

Some see gambling as just another form of entertainment. Just like a trip to the cinema, you pay some money and are entertained for a few hours. Gambling is different to other forms of entertainment, however. It revolves around money- the risk of losing money, and the desire to get more without having to work for it.

Hebrews 13:5 warns;

'Keep your lives free from the love of money and be content with what you have.'

Gambling can make money seem like the most important thing in life. Money can become an **idol**, as people substitute their worship of God with the worship of wealth instead. The first two of the Ten Commandments (**Exodus 20:3-4**) state that nothing should be worshipped other than God.

In **Matthew 6:24**, Jesus explains how love of money and love of God cannot go together.

'No one can serve two masters. Either he will hate the one and love the other, or he will be devoted to the one and despise the other. You cannot serve both God and Money.'

In this saying, Jesus talks about money as if it were a god that could be worshipped.

TPD

Do you think it is possible to worship money like a god? How would you put **Matthew 6:24** into your own words?

For some people, gambling can become an addiction. The risk and excitement of placing a bet releases chemicals which the brain demands more of. Like most addictions, gambling addiction causes severe problems for individuals and families. We sometimes read stories of people who gambled away their savings and left their families penniless or homeless because of their addiction.

It could be argued that gambling takes advantage of poor people. Many people who gamble cannot afford to do so. They spend what little they have on lottery tickets or scratch cards, hoping that they will win enough to get their family out of financial trouble. The temptation is often too great for those who are desperate, when in actual fact the chances of winning are extremely small.

Many forms of gambling trick people into giving up their money. Lotteries can be designed to fool people into thinking that they have a good chance of winning, when in fact the odds are incredibly low. Many casinos use sneaky techniques to manipulate the people that come through their doors. 'Amusements' try to attract teenagers by creating an exciting atmosphere of loud noise and flashing lights. It is said that Las Vegas Casinos do not have clocks or windows so the customers forget what time it is. They will lose track of how long they have been in the casino – and how much money they have spent!

MI
BC
SM

Make a poster warning teenagers about the dangers of gambling.

Com
MI
TPD
WO

Read the arguments below.

For

'Gambling is just another form of entertainment. Just like the cinema, you spend some money for a few hours fun. Even better than the cinema, you might win money!'

'The National Lottery is all about gambling, and they donate huge amounts of money to charity every year.'

'Just because a few people get addicted, doesn't mean everyone should have to stop.'

Against

'Gambling is designed to trick you into thinking you are going to win. Most people loose.'

'Gambling is not a responsible use of money. It should be spent on your family or on people who are in need. Gambling is just like throwing money away.'

'A lot of people find gambling addictive. They can end up losing all their money, or working up enormous debts. It doesn't just affect the gambler. It affects their family, and all of society.'

- In pairs, pick one partner to argue 'for', and one to argue 'against'.

- Take a few minutes to write down some arguments that you are going to use. You can use the arguments above, and anything else you can think of.

- Take it in turns to argue as strongly as possible for your side.

- Now, switch places and repeat the process, this time arguing for the opposite view.

- Discuss what you personally think about each view. What were the strongest arguments?

BC
TPD
SM
PD

Points Of View

Simon has started to spend a lot of time playing slot machines. He first played a slot machine while queueing in the chip shop, and liked the buzz he got. He then began spending more and more of his free time in the local 'amusements'. His dad is concerned that his son might become addicted.

List as many possible points of view for each of the following:

Simon:
For example:
• I'm definitely not addicted. I just like playing these machines.

Simon's dad:
For example:
• 'I'm worried that Simon might get addicted.'
• 'This is not a good way to waste money.'

The owner of a local 'amusements':

A lottery winner:

John, a recovering gambling addict:

John's wife:

Being content

It is often said that 'money can't buy you happiness'. We use money to buy food, clothes, and a place to live, but there are things that money can't buy. We shouldn't place too much importance on money.

TPD

Have you ever played 'Monopoly'? If you have, then you know how quickly you can loose enormous amounts of money.

Do you think that this side of 'Monopoly' is realistic?

The Bible reminds readers again and again that wealth does not last. Christians believe that it is better to find security by trusting God than by placing faith in money.

> 'Whoever trusts in his riches will fall, but the righteous will thrive like a green leaf.'
>
> **(Proverbs 11:28)**

It makes sense to make sure you have enough money to survive, and it is normal for people to want to own nice things. However, it can cause problems when we think that our happiness or success depends on how much money or possessions we have. This is sometimes called **consumerism** Jesus gives a warning to people who think this way:

> 'Then he said to them, 'Watch out! Be on your guard against all kinds of greed; a man's life does not consist in the abundance of his possessions.'
>
> **(Luke 12:15)**

'Mum! I want that!'

As a child, did you ever see a sweet or a toy that you wanted so much you felt like your happiness depended on it? The chances are, if you got what you wanted, it was soon eaten or lying forgotten in a toybox. You soon forgot how happy you thought it would make you, until you saw something else you wanted.

If you have ever felt like that, then you have experienced **consumerism** - the feeling that buying or owning a particular item will bring us happiness: 'If only I had that, then I'd be happy.'

All the major world religions, as well as common sense, tell us that our happiness can not depend on what we own.

Com
TPD
WO

Discuss in groups:

What is the latest 'must have' item? Is it an item of clothing, or technology?

Can you think of something that was 'must have' item, but is now out of fashion?

The main message about money in the Bible is that we should be content with what we already have. Paul sums up these feelings in **Philippians 4:11-12**:

> 'I am not saying this because I am in need, for I have learned to be content whatever the circumstances. I know what it is to be in need, and I know what it is to have plenty. I have learned the secret of being content in any and every situation, whether well fed or hungry, whether living in plenty or in want.'

Whether we have lots of money, or whether we have little, Christians believe that God always provides his followers with what they need for a happy, satisfied life. Rather than worrying about what we don't have, we can be thankful for what God has given us.

Com
TPD
WO

As a class, discuss what each of the following sayings tell us about money.

1. 'If you want to feel rich, just count the things you have that money can't buy' (Proverb).

2. 'A wise man should have money in his head, but not in his heart' (Jonathan Swift).

3. 'Wealth is not in having vast riches, it is in contentment' (The Prophet Muhammed).

4. 'I am opposed to millionaires, but it would be dangerous to offer me the position' (Mark Twain).

5. 'Charity looks at the need and not at the cause' (German proverb).

6. 'Charity begins at home, but should not end there' (Thomas Fuller).

Leisure

Leisure is what you do when you are not working or involved in other activities. It means being able to take time off from school or work and do what you want to do instead of what you must do.

Studies show that when people continually work for too many days in a row they become less productive. Their bodies and minds become less efficient as tiredness sets in.

Leisure is your time away from demands and duties when you can relax and feel at ease.

'I spend my free time sending text messages to my friends, playing hockey and reading novels. Schoolwork can be so stressful that it is important to take time to relax. On a Friday night some friends come round to my house and we watch a DVD and eat Chinese takeaway food. I really look forward to that after a hard week at school.'

MI
TPD
SM

My Perfect Weekend

How do you normally spend your free time at the weekend? Complete the following timetable in as much detail as you can.

Time	What I Do
Friday Night	
Saturday Morning	
Saturday Afternoon	
Saturday Evening	
Sunday Morning	
Sunday Afternoon	
Sunday Evening	

Changing times

Most people today have much more leisure time than they would have had in the past. In previous centuries even young people were forced to work, and quite often had to do fairly unpleasant jobs: cleaning chimneys, clearing out stables, working in factories and mills etc. Most people would have to work long and unsociable hours. Nowadays, people work an average of less than eight hours a day, which leaves a lot of time for relaxing.

ICT
SM

Use the internet or a library to research the type of jobs that young boys and girls had to do in previous centuries. Write a brief report sharing your findings with the class.

As you grow up, the way you spend your leisure time will change. Think about the activities you enjoyed as a young child compared with those which you like now. As a child your leisure time might have been organised by your parents or your teachers. As a teenager you will have more freedom to decide what to do with your spare time.

MI
TPD
SM

Our choice of leisure activities can bring many benefits. Some help us to keep fit, while others are a way of socialising with friends.

On the next page is a table listing popular leisure activities and the benefits of each activity.

Activities	Benefits
Football	To keep fit.
	To make new friends.
Swimming	It's good exercise.
	It helps me relax.
Cinema	To spend time with friends.
	It helps me relax.
Walking the dog	To do my parents a favour.
	I like to get outside.

Create a similar table for yourself.

In the left column list as many of your leisure activities as you can think of.

In the right column, explain your reasons for each activity.

In **groups of four** compare your tables.

1 How many of you share the same interests?

2 Does anyone have some unusual leisure activities?

Jesus' example

The Bible teaches that it is important to have a healthy balance between work and rest in life. It is vital that we take time to relax, refreshing the body and the mind.

Jesus knew the importance of rest, and the Bible records a number of times that Jesus would withdraw from busy crowds to be by himself. In **Mark 6:31** he invites his followers to do the same:

'Then, because so many people were coming and going that they did not even have a chance to eat, he said to them, 'Come with me by yourselves to a quiet place and get some rest.'

(Mark 6:31)

Clearly Jesus and his disciples were exhausted from their work. Jesus knew that it was time for them to rest for a few days. He called them to go away with him to an isolated place where they could relax.

If we work or study too hard without taking time to relax, it makes us less able to do our work well. It can even make you ill! The proper amount of time off makes people more keen to work, and better at what they do.

TPD SM What has been your favourite holiday? Write one or two pages describing your memories of this place and why you enjoyed going there.

Sabbath

Christians and Jews both follow the tradition of **Sabbath**. This means taking one day out of the week to worship God together and have complete rest. Jews celebrate Sabbath on Saturday, while most Christians worship on a Sunday to remember Jesus' **resurrection**.

This tradition goes back to the book of **Genesis**. After God had created the world, he took time to rest on the seventh day.

'By the seventh day God had finished the work he had been doing; so on the seventh day he rested from all his work. And God blessed the seventh day and made it holy, because on it he rested from the work of creating that he had done.'

(Genesis 2:2-3)

When it comes to giving the Ten Commandments, God instructs his people to rest one day in seven, just as he did.

'Remember the Sabbath day by keeping it holy. Six days you shall labour and do all your work, but the seventh day is a Sabbath to the Lord your God. On it you shall not do any work, neither you, nor your son or daughter, nor your manservant or maidservant, nor your animals, nor the alien within your gates. For in six days the Lord made the heavens and the earth, the sea, and all that is in them, but he rested on the seventh day. Therefore the Lord blessed the Sabbath day and made it holy.'

(Exodus 20:8-11)

When we think about the Ten Commandments, or any set of rules, we can sometimes feel that they are there to stop us doing what we want.

When the Ten Commandments were given, the people had just escaped from slavery in Egypt. These commandments told them how they were going to live from now on. Their new rules included: 'Everyone gets one day off every week'.

Imagine working as a slave. All day. Every day. Now imagine being told that from now on everyone would have a day off. In fact, it's the law.

Do you think this would be good news to slaves?

BC TPD SM

It has just been announced that from now on weekends are cancelled. Everyone will work and go to school seven days a week.

Write a diary entry describing how you feel about the decision.

Record how people's behaviour would be affected after; one week; one month, one year.

How would it change the world around you?

Christian attitudes vary regarding what is acceptable on Sunday. Many Christians follow God's example by resting completely on this day. They attend worship services, but they also keep a very strict view that any non-essential work is totally wrong. They keep Sunday special by choosing not to work, do household chores or go to the shops.

On the other hand, there are many Christians who go to church on Sunday, but see nothing wrong with playing sports, going out for lunch or doing the groceries.

MI TPD

What activities do some Christians avoid on the Sabbath?

Look at the list of leisure activities below and copy out the scale.

Where on the scale do you think each of the activities should be placed?

shopping	**church**
washing car	**Bible study**
hospital visit	**housework**
watching television	**cinema**
football	**ironing**
golf	**homework**
gardening	**sleeping**
playing with friends	**computer games**

Allowed   Not Allowed

⊢————————————————⊣

Eric Liddell was a sprinter and Rugby Union player from Scotland. His speed earned him the nickname 'The Flying Scotsman'.

Photograph provided by the Eric Liddell Centre.

In the 1924 Olympic games Eric's best event, the 100 metres, was to be held on Sunday. As a committed Christian, Eric refused to run on the Sabbath.

Instead he took part in the 400 metres race, which he was not expected to win. Not only did he win the race, but he broke the world record.

Eric Liddell's story was told in the 1981 film 'Chariots of Fire'.

Issues

Everybody needs to take a break from their work every now and then. We all know this from personal experience. Have you ever spent so long revising for a school test that you just don't seem to be able to see what is on the page any more? Have you ever been so tired that it feels as if your brain has stopped working altogether?

It should also be said that too much leisure time can make people feel bored and depressed. Doing nothing for days on end can make people feel lethargic and disinterested. For example, do you ever get fed up towards the end of the summer holidays?

Normally, our choice of leisure activities is just a matter of what we like. On other occasions deciding how we spend our leisure time becomes a **moral issue.**

FILMS

All films come with a certificate showing what age-group the film is appropriate for.

Some people don't think that film classifications are that important, but they are there for a good reason. A cinema that allows someone underage into a classified film has broken its license, and could be shut down.

ICT MI SM Find out exactly what each of the classifications mean. You can start by looking at the British Board of Film Classification website at **www.bbfc.co.uk**.

Com TPD Have you ever heard anyone boast about watching films that are classified for older viewers? Why do you think people would boast about this?

Another moral issue connected with films is the sale of illegally copied DVDs. If you buy an illegal copy of a film, you shouldn't just be worried about poor sound and picture quality.

1 Buying **pirate** DVDs can fund other criminal activities like drug dealing.

2 Selling pirate DVDs is a criminal offence. In one year 246 people were charged and found guilty. 116 were sent to prison.

A police raid on an illegal DVD factory.

Pictures provided by the Industry Trust.

3 Pirated DVDs costs the country £100 million per year in tax- money that would have gone into health and education, rather than into criminal's pockets.

SPORT

Regular exercise is beneficial, and taking part in sport also teaches us the importance of commitment, self-discipline and good teamwork. For Christians, it is the ideal opportunity to be a good example by showing sportsmanship to fellow players.

Being part of a sports team can put great demands on time. Many sportsmen and women give up most of their free time in the evenings and at weekends. There is a danger that other activities such as study or spending time with family and other friends can get pushed aside. Christian players must be careful that sports do not become central to their lives. While it is rewarding to be dedicated to a team, it is important that Christians place God first.

VIDEO GAMES

Com
TPD
WO
PD

Video Games And Violence

'With the number of violent video games and movies out there, it is no wonder that violent crime is on the rise.'

'Scientific studies have failed to show any link between violent crime and video games.'

'Some video games are very like the simulators that I used in my military training. Video games train young people to be killers. They desensitise our minds to violence and killing.'

'Video games are just games. Anyone who goes out and does something like this in real life should be locked up. There's a big difference between gamers and murderers!'

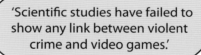

Using the voices above as a starting point, organise a class debate on this topic:

Does violence in video games, TV and movies lead to violence in real life?

MUSIC

People enjoy all different kinds of music. Music can make us feel happy or sad, relaxed or excited. It is good to be aware of how your choice of music makes you feel.

As with films and television, all music comes with a message. Some would argue that it can dangerous to listen to songs or artists with bad moral values.

TPD

What is your favourite song at the moment?

How does it make you feel?

Write down the lyrics of the song. What message does it give?

It is important to be careful of the message that comes with entertainment. For example, is it beneficial to watch horror films in which young people are being murdered? Is it wise for Christians to watch television programmes in which God is being criticised or ridiculed?

The Bible's teaching on this is straightforward:

'Hate what it is evil; cling to what is good'

(**Romans 12:9**)

You can buy music on CD or purchase it online. Some musicians make songs available for free on their websites.

Downloading music without paying, and without the permission of the artist, is called **music piracy**.

BC
TPD
SM
PD

A Matter of Opinion?

Rick is a huge fan of the band Gujarat. He loves all their songs, and goes to concerts as often as he can. Gujarat's new album 'Outgoing Post' has just been released, but Rick has no money. He decides to go online and download the music illegally.

List as many possible points of view for each of the following:

Rick:
For example:
• 'I really like this band. I've bought loads of their stuff. They probably owe me one little album.'

The website owner:
For example:
• 'Record companies make millions of pounds, and most doesn't even go to the musician. People are free to download whatever they like.'

Carl, lead singer of Gujarat:

The owner of the record company:

The law:

MI
TPD

1 What different pieces of advice does the Bible give about leisure?

2 Explain why Sunday is an important day for Christians.

3 What questions should a Christian ask when deciding on a particular leisure activity?

4 What are the positive effects of playing sports?

5 Are there any dangers associated with playing sports?

6 a What kinds of entertainment do you enjoy?
  b Do you think that any of these are harmful?

7 Is there any form of entertainment you find offensive? Explain why.

The Environment

When we hear the word **environment** we often think of news reports about pollution, melting ice caps, oil slicks or holes in the ozone layer. These are important issues to consider. We should also be aware of the wonder of the world – animals, plants, birds, oceans, trees and other things around us.

Where did the Earth come from?

1 The Big Bang

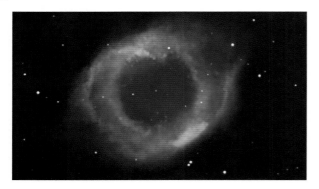

First proposed by Georges Lemaître, the big bang theory explains the beginnings of the universe when all of space exploded out from an infinitely small point. All of the stars and planets, including the Earth, were formed during the following expansion of the universe, which is still continuing today.

ICT
SM

Use the internet or a library to find out about Georges Lemaître.

• What was his job?

• What was the big bang theory originally called?

2 Evolution

The theory of evolution seeks to explain the origin of life on Earth. In simple terms, it describes how more advanced forms of life such as human beings have slowly developed from simple organisms. The most famous scientist to propose a theory of evolution was Charles Darwin, who in 1859 published his book *On The Origin Of Species*. He argued that life began with very simple cells and developed into what we see today: birds, fish,

3 Genesis

The first chapters of the book of Genesis explain how the universe was created by God. Christians believe that, far from coming into existence by accident, the universe was made by God with a purpose. Genesis describes how God made the world and everything in it in six days: the sun, the moon, animals, plants, seas. Finally, God creates humans 'in his own image'. On the seventh day God rested.

MI
BC
SM
Read the creation story in **Genesis 1:1-2:3** and draw a comic strip illustrating the different stages of creation.

- Your comic should have at least seven panels
- Make sure that it is colourful and eye-catching.
- Include a short caption for each panel explaining what is happening.

The Genesis creation story is part of the Jewish and Christian scriptures. Muslims have a similar story which is found in sections throughout the Qur'an.

Some Christians believe that the Genesis story should be read literally. In other words, the Bible tells exactly how the world was created over a period of six days. They do not believe the theory of evolution.

Others argue that the Bible cannot be read like a science textbook. They believe that the world was created by God for a purpose, but have no problem believing in evolution or the big bang. The Bible explains **why** God created the world, and not necessarily **how** he did so.

ICT
MI
How much can you find out about the Muslim version of the creation story?

MI
TPD
SM
Read **Genesis 1:1 - 2:3** and answer the following questions.

1 What was God's last and most important creation?

2 What did God say about each thing that he created?

3 What did God do on the seventh day?

4 Name two responsibilities God gave to human beings.

5 Why did God create the universe? Read the following verses to find two reasons:

- **Colossians 1:6**
- **Revelation 4:11**
- **Isaiah 43:7**

Com
WO
Read the following statement and discuss it as a class:

'Michelangelo spent over three years painting the story of Creation on the six thousand square feet ceiling of the Sistine Chapel, yet some Christians actually believe that God brought the entire earth into existence from nothing in only six days.'

Responsibility for the Environment

The Old Testament teaches that the earth belongs to God:

'The earth is the Lord's, and everything in it, the world, and all who live in it; for he founded it upon the seas and established it upon the waters.'

(Psalm 24:1)

In Genesis we see humanity being given the job of caring for the world around us.

'The Lord God took the man and put him in the Garden of Eden to work it and take care of it.'

(Genesis 2:15)

The Bible also gives specific advice on caring for the environment, for example, instructions for growing crops. The land was not to be planted one year in every seven:

'Let the land keep a Sabbath for the Lord.'

(Leviticus 25:2)

No crops at all were to be sown or reaped for one year in every fifty.

'The fiftieth year shall be a jubilee for you; do not sow and do not reap what grows of itself or harvest the untended vines. For it is a jubilee and is to be holy for you; eat only what is taken directly from the fields.'

(Leviticus 25:11-12)

Farmers today know the wisdom of leaving a field unplanted or **fallow** for a season. Being careful with resources and allowing the land to rest means better harvests in the future.

Pollution

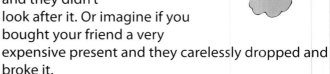

Think for a moment about how upset you would be if you spent a great deal of time making somebody a gift and they didn't look after it. Or imagine if you bought your friend a very expensive present and they carelessly dropped and broke it.

Taking that into consideration, how do you think God reacts when he sees how some human beings treat this planet? How do you feel when you think about how people pollute the atmosphere, vandalise areas of natural beauty and dump rubbish everywhere?

MI
TPD
WO

Types of Pollution

There are a number of different types of pollution that can dramatically damage the environment.

Get into groups of **four** or **five**. Discuss how much you know about the following kinds of pollution, and write your ideas down on a large sheet of blank paper. If nobody in your group knows about any of these things, try to guess what they might be.

1. Air pollution.
2. Water pollution.
3. Global warming / Climate change.
4. The ozone layer.
5. Acid rain.
6. E-waste.
7. Conservation.

The Bible commands people to be responsible for the world around them. We can be responsible by keeping up to date with current research and facts about the environment. This information should help you understand the various ways in which our world is being damaged.

1 Air Pollution

Certain types of factories release chemicals into the air which can be extremely harmful to the environment and the atmosphere. These chemicals can cause damage hundreds of miles away from where they were originally released. This causes air pollution or smog, which has been linked to serious diseases such as cancer.

2 Water Pollution

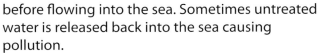

Water is essential for drinking, washing dishes and clothes, bathing and flushing the toilet. Used water leaves our homes through sewers, and is processed in a sewage treatment works before flowing into the sea. Sometimes untreated water is released back into the sea causing pollution.

If people bury rubbish in illegal landfills, poisonous liquids can enter the ground. This can damage plant life and enter underground water supplies where it pollutes people's drinking water. Many of the world's poorest areas do not have clean drinking water, resulting in sickness and a low life expectancy.

3 Global Warming and Climate Change

The amount of carbon dioxide gas in the air has increased greatly over the last century because more people are driving cars. The use of electricity, oil and natural gas has also increased. This causes high levels of carbon dioxide to enter the Earth's atmosphere, which adds to the **greenhouse effect**. This is when heat gets trapped within the atmosphere, affecting the weather dramatically. This results in tornadoes, drought, flooding and forest fires. The heat is causing the ice caps to melt which some say will cause the sea level to rise. Any animals who cannot cope with these environmental changes will die out.

4 The Ozone Layer

This is a layer in the Earth's upper atmosphere which protects people from the harmful rays of the sun. It is damaged by CFC gases, which in the past were used in fridges and aerosol cans. The famous 'hole' in the ozone layer is over the Antarctic, approximately ten miles across. Damage caused can last for one hundred years, which is why there is an international ban on the use of CFCs. There is evidence that this ban is helping the ozone layer, yet some countries still use CFCs in their products because they are cheap.

5 Acid Rain

Harmful gases such as sulphur dioxide are produced by cars, factory chimneys and oil or coal power stations. Once in the atmosphere these gases combine with water to produce **acid rain**. This rain is extremely harmful to the environment: it kills trees, plants and fish, and can even damage buildings.

6 E-Waste

Technology is moving forward incredibly quickly: everyone wants to own the most up to date mobile phone or computer; but what happens to all the old equipment? The result is **electronic waste**, or e-waste.

Unwanted computers, mobiles and other electronic gadgets are often sold on to poorer countries, but many of them do not work. Workers are paid a tiny wage to remove useful electronic components. The conditions are terrible and workers are exposed to poisonous fumes.

Equipment that cannot be sold on is dumped into landfill sites. This means digging up parts of the countryside and packing it full of waste. Computer and television screens contain lead which is poisonous.

E-waste is one of the fastest growing problems in pollution. The UK produces fifty million tonnes every year.

ICT
BC
WO

Use the internet or a library to find out more about these forms of pollution.

In groups of **four** pick one pollution issue that you find interesting. Design and create a poster explaining the issue to others.

TPD
WO

Get into groups of **three** or **four**, and try and think of as many different uses as you can for the following items:

1 Cardboard boxes.
2 Plastic milk cartons.
3 Glass jars.
4 Newspapers.
5 Plastic bags.

What can I do?

It does not take a great deal of effort to be environmentally friendly. Firstly, we can remember not to drop litter or spit out chewing gum onto the ground. These little things can make a big difference to our planet's health.

Secondly, we can recycle as much as possible. We can take glass containers to a bottle bank and donate old and unwanted clothes to charity shops.

Most

households will have a blue bin for the following materials:

- Aluminium cans.
- Plastic bottles.
- Newspapers and magazines.
- Cardboard packets, tissue rolls, cereal boxes etc.

You can also **reuse** different household materials rather than throwing them into the bin.

Lastly, we can be more sensible around the house and remember to switch off appliances and lights when they are not in use. Not only will our electricity bills go down, but most of our electricity is produced by burning fuel which pollutes the atmosphere. The less electricity we waste, the less pollution we are responsible for.

MI
BC
TPD
SM

Read the following story and answer the questions at the end.

The School Formal

Sonia was really excited about the school formal. Since she was in Year 8 she had heard people talking excitedly about how sixth form girls were invited to a special party. Now she was in her last year of school it was finally her turn to go! She couldn't wait.

Sonia had been to the hairdresser that afternoon. It cost a fortune but she didn't care. You only go to your school formal once, she reasoned. She ran into her room, turned on her stereo, then went into the en-suite bathroom. She turned the radiator up so the room wouldn't be cold when she got out of the shower, then opened the window so the mirror would not steam up from the heat.

Sonia turned on the shower and ran downstairs. Her mother had made her a sandwich but she was too preoccupied with the evening ahead, so she took a few bites and left the rest. She ran upstairs again, into the bathroom, armed with three dry

towels, shower gel, deodorant, body spray and perfume.

By now the shower was really warm, so she washed quickly, careful not to get her hair wet. As she put on her make-up she noticed that her hair was a little out of place. She plugged in her hair straighteners and put some gel on her hair.

The phone rang. It was Donna. 'Are you ready yet?' she chirped, enthusiastically. 'How's your hair?'

The conversation went on for ten minutes as they discussed hair, make-up and their dresses.

Sonia finished the phone call. She noticed that she had left the shower running. She turned it off and put on her dress. Perfect. A quick spray of perfume and she was ready to go.

Oh, wait! Her hair! She grabbed the straighteners which by now were on full power. She spent a few minutes fixing her fringe, using hairspray to keep it in place.

Sonia went downstairs, leaving her stereo blaring. She asked her Dad to give her a lift to the hotel where the formal was happening. It was just a mile away from their house.

'Take the big car, Daddy,' she pleaded. 'I don't want to arrive in Mum's old banger.'

Sonia's father rolled his eyes. 'Anything for a quiet life,' he thought. He went out and started the car's engine.

'Put the heater on in the car, Daddy!' Sonia shouted out the open front door. 'I'm just going to take one last look at myself. I'll only be a few minutes!'

1 Make a list of all of the ways in which Sonia was environmentally unfriendly. Explain why each action was harmful to the environment.

2 If Sonia was more environmentally aware, how might her behaviour have changed? Rewrite the story to make Sonia more considerate and responsible.

MI
TPD
SM

Which of your activities could be environmentally unfriendly?

Think through your normal day from getting up to going to sleep. List any activities that could be environmentally unfriendly.

What could you change?

Responses

In the very first chapter of the Bible we read that human beings were created to be in charge of the Earth, to look after it and everything that lives in it.

> 'Then God said, 'Let us make man in our image, in our likeness, and let them rule over the fish of the sea and the birds of the air, over the livestock, over all the earth, and over all the creatures that move along the ground.'
>
> **(Genesis 1:26)**

When we read this and when we hear about the many different kinds of pollution that humanity is causing, there are a number of different responses.

1 Selfishness

We could choose to ignore the problems of pollution and our responsibility for the Earth. We want an easy life and don't want to be troubled about the environment. In **Genesis 3:17** we read how the selfishness of Adam and Eve caused the environment to be cursed.

> 'To Adam he said, 'Because you listened to your wife and ate from the tree about which I commanded you, 'You must not eat of it,'
>
> Cursed is the ground because of you; through painful toil you will eat of it all the days of your life.'
>
> **(Genesis 3:17)**

2 Thankfulness

The Bible is full of people praising God for his creation and good works. The **Psalms** are examples of how God's people were very thankful for the world in which they lived:

'Sing to the Lord with thanksgiving; make music to our God on the harp. He covers the sky with clouds; he supplies the earth with rain and makes grass grow on the hills. He provides food for the cattle and for the young ravens when they call.'

(Psalm 147:7-9)

Churches today continue to celebrate God's creation with hymns and songs. They remind people of the wonderful world that God has made. Many churches respond to God's creation by holding celebration services at harvest time each year. Churches are decorated with flowers, fruit and vegetables, and worship services are held to praise and thank God for the wonder of his world.

3 Responsibility

Following God's command in **Genesis**, many Christians talk about what it means to be a good **steward** of creation. Look at the following definitions:

Steward – A person who carefully looks after something that is not theirs.

Stewardship – The responsibility to control the earth, to cultivate it and to guard it.

Being a good steward means looking after the earth and controlling the way in which we use our resources. We must stop polluting our planet and start respecting what we have been given.

This will not only benefit us, but also those future generations who will live on this planet after us.

BC TPD WO	Design a class project showing care and responsibility for the environment.

In **pairs** come up with a suggestion about what you class project could be.

- You could make a compost heap in your school grounds.
- You could make sure all the school's scrap paper is recycled.
- You could replace school bins with separate containers for plastic, cans, paper and organic waste.
- You could plant a tree.

Present your idea to the class. When all the ideas have been presented have a class vote to decide what project you are going to do.

Glossary

Please note that the definitions given below relate to the work covered in this textbook. Some words may also have alternative meanings, eg 'contract'.

Absolute moral standards: Rules for life that never change

Abstention: To refrain from an activity, such as drinking alcohol

Adam and Eve: In the book of Genesis, Adam and Eve are the first human beings created by God

Addicted: To become dependent on a habit or substance

AIDS: Acquired Immune Deficiency Syndrome. A condition leaving the body open to attack by infection or tumours

Blended Family: Families where one or both parents have divorced and remarried. May include children from two families

Celibate: Refraining from sexual activity

Conscience: An inner sense of right and wrong

Consumerism: The idea that buying or owning material goods can bring happiness or fulfilment

Copyright: Law which protects music, writing, films and art from being stolen or copied

Dependent: Relying on someone else

Discrimination: Treating people differently because of their gender, race, religion or background

E-waste: Electronic equipment which has been thrown away

Egoistic: Self-centred

Escalation: When something like anger or violence gets increasingly worse

Ethnic Minority: A group of people of a certain race, religion or nationality living in a country where most people belong to a different race, religion or nationality

Exclusion: When someone is left out of a group

Extended Family: A family unit of mother, father, children, grandparents, aunts, uncles and cousins

Fallow: When a field is left unplanted, to allow the soil to recover

Gender: Male or Female

Gentile: Non-Jewish

Golden Rule: 'Do unto others as you would have them do unto you.'

Greenhouse effect: Heat trapped inside Earth's atmosphere changes the weather dramatically

Heterosexual: Being sexually attracted to the opposite gender

Holocaust: Mass killing of Jews and other groups by the Nazis

Homophobia: Hatred or abuse directed towards homosexuals

Homosexual: Being sexually attracted to the same gender

Hypocrite: Someone who pretends to have certain beliefs, but does not act on them

Idol: Something which is worshipped in the place of God

Independent: Not relying on others

Insecurity: A lack of confidence in yourself

Integrated education: Schools that educate Protestant and Catholic pupils together

Job Seeker's Allowance: Money that the government gives to people who are unemployed

Landfill site: When large amounts of rubbish are buried in the soil

Low self-esteem: Having a low opinion of yourself, or feeling worthless

Marginalised: When people are given less value and treated with less importance

Media: Television, film, newspapers and magazines

Moderate: Keeping within reasonable limits

Morality: A code of conduct based on ideas of right and wrong

Multiculturalism: When many different cultures exist within one society

Music piracy: Illegally downloading or copying music

Narcissistic: Vain and self-interested

Nuclear Family: Basic family unit of mother, father and children

Obedience: Following rules and teachings

Ozone layer: A layer in the atmosphere that filters harmful rays from the sun

Passive smoking: When someone breathes in the harmful smoke from someone else's cigarette

Peer group: A group of friends, usually of the same age

Peer pressure: Pressure from friends to behave in a way similar to them

Persecution: Abuse or punishment or a group of people, usually because of religion

Pharisees: Jewish religious leaders at the time of Jesus, who had many strict rules

Psalms: Spiritual songs or poems, such as the Book of Psalms in the Bible

Poverty: Not having enough money or resources to meet basic needs

Prejudice: An assumption based on very little knowledge

Prophesying: Speaking God's word

Qu'ran: The holy book of Islam

Racism: Prejudice or discrimination based on someone's race

Rebellion: Disobedience towards authority

Reconciliation: Bringing together people or groups that had been split apart

Relative moral standards: Rules for life that change according to the situation

Respect: Thinking highly of someone, and treating them well

Sabbath: A day set aside for rest and worship

Samaritan: Someone from Samaria

Sectarianism: Conflict between two groups within the same religion

Self-conscious: Being uncomfortable with yourself and very concerned with what others think of you

Self-esteem: Your opinion of yourself

Self-Image: The picture we have of ourselves

Sexism: When someone is treated unfairly because of their gender

Sexual orientation: The gender to which someone is attracted.

Single-Parent Family: A family unit with children brought up by one parent

Socialise: Mixing with other people

Soul: The spiritual part of human beings, often believed to survive death

Spiritual: The part of a human being which is not physical

Stereotype: A fixed idea about what someone or something is like

Steward: Someone who looks after something which is not theirs

Stewardship: The responsibility to care for the Earth

Suffrage: The right to vote

Talents: Our skills and abilities. Also, a coin at the time of Jesus.

Unemployed: When a person does not have a job

Unique: The only one of its kind

Values: A set of morals or beliefs

Vocation: A sense of 'calling' to a particular job

Wider Family: Families or friends who share a house and live like one family

Acknowledgements

The authors and Colourpoint Books gratefully acknowledge the assistance of the following people and organisations:

Open Doors

The Industry Trust, especially Katy Carter

Fairtrade, especially Joanna Brightwell

The Eric Liddell Centre

Joni and Friends

Derrick Phillips at WriterSite

Picture credits:

Martin Gilbride: 19, 73

Juliana Gilbride: 122

McNeice family: 44

Liz Milligan: 66

Fransuer Mukula: 79

Sam Kennedy: 95

Noreen Kennedy: 95

Norman Johnston: 51, 77

iStockphoto: cover and frontispiece, 5 (bottom right), 15 (top right), 23, 26 (right), 28, 29 (top left), 36, 40 (four images), 43 (right), 49 (bottom left), 53 (right), 67 (left), 72 (left), 73, 81, 89, 91, 106, 107, 108 (right), 113 (left), 115 (bottom left), 115 (top right original source), 116 (left), 117, 119 (bottom right), 122

Wikimedia commons: 21, 75, 76 (top left and top right), 96, 99, 104, 109 (three images, right), 116 (right and bottom left)

Juliana Gilbride

Special thanks goes to Michael Spence and Ross Thompson for their hard work as editors and to Sheila for giving me the challenge of another book. For Martin, Tom and Kate.

Heather Hamilton

I want to acknowledge the hard work of everyone at Colourpoint during the production of this book and the entire series. Their expertise and vision has made my first experience as an author a very positive one. Thanks are also due to Richard Hamilton for his encouragement and support. For Richard, Reuben and Nathan.

Copyright Information

Also in this series

Also available in this series of resources for the new Core Syllabus for Religious Education at Key Stage 3:

Christianity in Close-up Book 1
THE REVELATION OF GOD
by Wendy Faris and Heather Hamilton

ISBN: 978 1 904242 75 8
Price: £11.99

Christianity in Close-up Book 2
THE CHRISTIAN CHURCH
by Wendy Faris and Heather Hamilton
ISBN: 978 1 90424276 5
Price: £9.99
In the same accessible and colourful format as Book 1, these texts include questions and activities which address the topics in a fresh and engaging style, helping to create active participation and enjoyment of the subject.

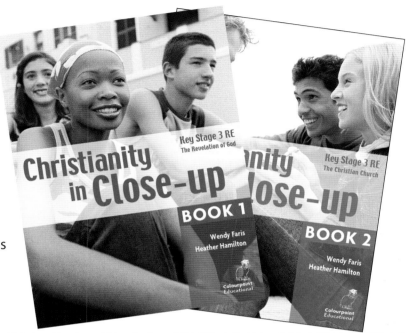

Resource CDs

A CD of printable activity sheets and teacher resources is available for each book. These can be printed out in the necessary numbers and distributed to the class. There are also sheets specifically for teachers which provide resources for a variety of additional practical activities.

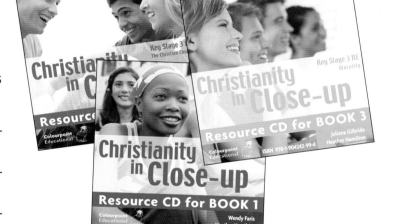

Resource CD for Book 1
ISBN: 978 1 904242 85 7   *Price: £39.99 + VAT*

Resource CD for Book 2
ISBN: 978 1 904242 86 4   *Price: £29.99 + VAT*

Resource CD for Book 3
ISBN: 978 1 904242 99 4   *Price: £29.99 + VAT*

Contact Colourpoint Educational at:
Tel: **028 9182 6339**   Fax: **028 9182 1900**
Web: **www.colourpoint.co.uk**

All orders to MiMO Distribution:
Tel: **028 9182 0505**   E-mail: **sales@mimodistribution.co.uk**

Colourpoint Books, Colourpoint House, Jubilee Business Park,
21 Jubilee Road, Newtownards, Co Down, BT23 4YH

Colourpoint
Educational
SERVING EDUCATION